# Writing Skills, G[...]

## Contents

# Introduction

Language expression is an important skill for students to master. Learning to write helps students to interact with the larger world. It helps them to construct personal meaning and to communicate personal experiences. Writing well is the foundation for success in most school subjects.

One way to learn to write better is through imitation. *Writing Skills* gives students practice in reading and writing different types of papers. Students read original papers written by experienced writers, respond to what they read, analyze what they read, plan and organize writing ideas, write and revise drafts, and practice self-assessment. In addition, students have the opportunities to apply instructional standards, refresh their writing and language skills, build their confidence as writers, and prepare for standardized writing tests.

## Standards for English Language Arts

The National Council of Teachers of English (NCTE) has stressed that "all students must have the opportunities and resources to develop the language skills they need to pursue life's goals and to participate fully as informed, productive members of society." The NCTE also states that students need to "apply a wide range of strategies as they write and use different writing process elements appropriately to communicate with different audiences for a variety of purposes." This book helps students to practice a variety of writing strategies. To learn more about the NCTE's twelve standards for the development of creative and innovative Language Arts curricula and instruction, visit **http://www.ncte.org/standards/**.

## Organization

The book is divided into nine units. Each unit deals with a different type of writing. Each unit has seven parts. First, students read a Model Paper. Then, they Respond to the Model Paper. Next, they Analyze the Model Paper. After they have studied the model paper, they begin the process of writing their own paper. They receive a Writing Assignment, which includes a graphic organizer. A page is provided for the students to begin their First Draft. Once the first draft is complete, they begin to Revise the Draft. Then, they evaluate their own work or that of a classmate using a Writing Report Card.

## Diagnostic Writing Prompt and Sample Papers

When you begin a writing program with your class, an informal assessment of students' writing skills helps you determine their initial strengths and weaknesses. Use the narrative prompt below to obtain diagnostic anchor papers for your class. Evaluate these papers using the Scoring Rubric on page 4. Before you begin the evaluation process, you may want to examine the sample papers and commentaries (pages 6–15). The papers are examples of student writing at each level of the rubric. The commentaries provide explanations of why each paper received its rating. All the sample papers are assigned a value from 4 to 1 using the Scoring Rubric on page 4.

Ask students to discuss or use their own paper to respond to the following questions:

1. What is the best thing that has ever happened to you?
2. When and where did it happen?
3. What made it so special?

Then, read the following directions aloud: *Write a story describing the best thing that ever happened to you. Give details that help your readers to imagine the story you tell.*

Encourage students to plan before writing their narrative. Suggest that they list the main ideas they will write about. Tell them to put the main ideas in the order they will write about them. Remind students to give details that support each main idea.

## Proofreading Symbols

A chart of proofreading symbols is included on page 16. Students are encouraged to use these symbols as they edit and revise drafts. You may want to post the proofreading symbols as a ready reference for students.

## Scoring Student Writing

Many states now include writing assessments in their statewide testing programs. The evaluation of these assessments often relies upon a state-specific scoring rubric. You may use your state's scoring rubric to evaluate your students' writing performance and progress. If your state does not provide a rubric, you may use the 4-point Scoring Rubric on page 4 that was used to evaluate the sample papers provided in this book. Still another option is the *6 + 1 Traits™ of Analytic Writing Assessment Scoring Guide*. This guide and sample student papers that have been evaluated using this guide can be found at **http://www.nwrel.org/assessment/**.

## Writing Conference Record

A Writing Conference Record can be found on page 5. Questions and directions in the record help you evaluate each student's writing process skills and determine performance objectives. Records are used within the context of student-teacher conferences. Conferences promote dialogue about the writing experience and prompt discussion of ideas for writing, critical analysis, and opportunities for reading aloud. Conferences also help distinguish writing as a purposeful and rewarding activity.

## Additional Writing Prompts

Additional writing prompts for each kind of writing are included below. These prompts can be used to give students additional writing practice in one or more kinds of writing. They can also be used as reinforcement in other instructional settings, in learning centers, and for homework. Encourage students to use writing plans to organize their thoughts and notes before writing a draft.

## Personal Narrative

1. You've attended different schools over the years. Think about a time when you started a new school. This could be kindergarten or middle school, or anywhere in between. How did you feel on the first day at your new school? Did anyone make you feel welcome? Write a narrative describing your experiences at the new school. Be sure to include any problems that you encountered and tell how you overcame them.

2. Think of the worst thing that ever happened to you. When did it happen? Where were you? What made it so awful? Write a story describing the worst thing that ever happened to you. Be sure to include details that help your readers picture the events in the story.

3. You make decisions every day, some small, some large. Think about an important decision that you've had to make. How did you make the decision? How was your life different after you made the decision? What might have happened if you'd made another choice? Write a story about your decision and how it affected your life.

4. Courage comes in many forms. There is physical courage, as when a person helps someone in a dangerous situation. And there is moral courage, when you do something that you know is right, even when it's hard. Think of a time that you were courageous. What happened? What did you do? What made you act? What was the result? Write a story describing this event. Include vivid details that make your story come alive.

## Descriptive Story

1. Do you have a favorite family holiday? Use that holiday as the subject of a descriptive story. Use words to describe what you see, hear, feel, taste, and smell.

2. Think about your last trip to a movie theater. Make notes about the things that you saw, heard, touched, smelled, and tasted there. Use your notes to write a story using the theater as a setting. Use as many descriptive words as you can. Include at least three similes and three metaphors.

3. Look through the real estate ads in your local paper. Find an ad that interests you. Imagine the house and the people who are selling it. What is the house like? What are the people like? Why are they selling the house? Write a story describing the house and why it is for sale. Remember to use descriptions based on your five senses.

4. Imagine you are camping in a forested area. The Sun is shining through the trees, but a summer storm is on the way. Make notes about what you see, hear, feel, smell, and taste as you wait for the storm. Write a story using this setting.

## How-to Paper

1. Think of a park or restaurant near your house. Make notes about the streets and turns that you use to get there. Then, write step-by-step directions for getting from your house to this location. As the final step, tell what you will do when you get there.

2. Think of your favorite meal. Imagine that you are going to cook this meal and serve it to your best friend. What steps will you take? What ingredients will you need? How about pots and pans? Write a how-to paper outlining the steps you will follow as you prepare this meal.

3. Tests. You can't get away from them. But there are ways that you can get ready for tests. Jot down all the things that you can do to prepare for a test. Then, interview your classmates and teachers for additional ideas. Finally, write a paper describing how to study for a test.

4. You probably celebrate several holidays during the year. Think of your favorite holiday and all the traditions and decorations that accompany it. Then, write a paper describing how to celebrate this holiday.

## Compare and Contrast Paper

1. Think about the music you like to listen to. How is it like the music that your parents enjoy? How is it different? Write a paper that compares and contrasts the two types of music.

2. Choose two vehicles that you would like to drive. Use your library, the Internet, and other resources to gather information about the vehicles. Then, write a paper that explains their similarities and differences.

3. Think about a character in one of your favorite books. What does he or she like to do? What is he or she good at? What kinds of problems does he or she have to overcome? Write a paper that compares and contrasts this character with yourself.

4. What are your two favorite TV shows? The next time you watch the shows, take notes about the characters, plots, and settings. Then, write a paper that tells how the two shows are alike and how they are different.

## Short Report

1. Do you spend much time at the movies? Find out more about how movies are made. Where do the ideas come from? Who builds the sets, controls the lights, and creates the special effects? How do they do their jobs? Use your library, the Internet, and other resources to learn how movies are made. Share what you learn in a short report.

2. Your community has a history all its own. Use reference materials, including local historians and newspapers, to learn more about the important events in your community's history. Then, share the information in a short report.

3. Money can't buy you love, but it does buy many other things that you want or need. Research the history of money. Then, write a report telling how money has changed over time.

4. Everyone has heard of Thomas Edison and Benjamin Franklin, but what about the millions of other inventors who have changed our world? Use your library, the Internet, and other resources to learn about inventors such as Grace Hopper and Elijah McCoy. Then, write a short report so others can learn about them, too.

## Persuasive Writing

1. Think about your favorite game or sport. What makes it so special? Write a persuasive essay to convince your friends to play the game.

2. Parents and teachers at your school have asked the school board to stop selling sodas and candy in vending machines and in the cafeteria. They say students should eat more nutritious foods. What is your opinion? Write a persuasive essay for the school newspaper to convince others that your opinion is the right one.

3. A group of skateboarders has petitioned the city council to turn your neighborhood park into a skateboard park. What do you think about this idea? Write a persuasive essay expressing your opinion.

4. Have you seen a movie recently that didn't live up to all the hype? What made it so bad? Write a movie review persuading others not to see the movie. Support your opinion with examples and details from the movie.

5. Many people believe that everyone should learn at least one language other than English. What is your opinion? Should students be required to learn a foreign language in order to graduate from high school? Write a persuasive letter to your principal stating your opinion. Be sure to support your opinion with examples and details.

# Scoring Rubric for Writing

## Score of 4
**The student's response ...**

- <u>clearly and completely</u> addresses the writing task,

- demonstrates an understanding of the purpose for writing,

- maintains a single focus,

- presents a central idea supported by relevant details and explanations,

- uses paragraphs to organize main ideas and supporting details under the umbrella of the central idea,

- presents content in a logical order or sequence,

- uses variety in sentence types and lengths,

- uses language appropriate to the writing task, such as language rich with sensory details in a model of descriptive writing,

- summarizes main ideas in a concluding paragraph in a model of expository or persuasive writing,

- establishes and defends a position in a model of persuasive writing, and

- has few or no errors in the standard rules of English grammar, punctuation, capitalization, and spelling.

## Score of 3
**The student's response ...**

- <u>generally</u> follows the criteria described above, and

- has some errors in the standard rules of English grammar, punctuation, capitalization, and spelling, but not so many that a reader's comprehension is impaired.

## Score of 2
**The student's response ...**

- <u>marginally</u> follows the criteria described above, and

- has several errors in the standard rules of English grammar, punctuation, capitalization, and spelling that may impair a reader's comprehension.

## Score of 1
**The student's response ...**

- <u>fails</u> to follow the criteria described above, and

- has numerous and serious errors in the standard rules of English grammar, punctuation, capitalization, and spelling that impair a reader's comprehension.

# Writing Conference Record

Encourage each student to share a writing sample with you. Then complete the conference record below. Invite each student to participate in several writing conferences. Use the records to assess each student's skills and progress.

Student's Name _____ Date _____

Title of the Writing Sample discussed today: _____

## Kind of writing this sample represents:

☐ Personal Narrative     ☐ How-to Paper     ☐ Persuasive Letter

☐ Narrative     ☐ Compare and Contrast Paper     ☐ Persuasive Movie Review

☐ Descriptive Story     ☐ Short Report     ☐ Persuasive Essay

| Questions or Directions | Student's Responses and Teacher's Notes |
|---|---|
| What were your writing goals for this paper? | |
| Why did you choose this kind of writing? | |
| Why did you choose this topic? | |
| How did you organize your ideas and notes for this paper? | |
| Describe the writing process you used to write this paper, including revising your draft. | |
| What do you like most about this paper? | |
| In general, what is your strongest writing skill? | |
| Which writing skill do you think you need to improve? How will you do it? | |

Date of next writing conference: _____

Writing Skills 8, SV 6508-0

# Diagnostic Sample Narratives

The following sample represents a narrative that meets the criteria for a 4-point paper.

## The Best Thing Ever!

My mom is in the military. When Mom left for a six-month tour of duty I had to stay with my uncle. I really missed my mom, but there wasn't much I could do about it. One night I was sitting on the couch watching television when my uncle said, "Guess what! In one month you're going to take a plane to see your mother in Hawaii." I leapt off the couch in excitement and ran upstairs to my room. I jumped on my bed, giggling and talking to myself all evening.

On September 7, my uncle and I went to the airport. There were kids everywhere. Some were in line, but most of them were running around and chattering like monkeys. Once we got our tickets, we were packed into a little, hot waiting room. I was sweating and breathing heavily as I waited for my turn to board the plane. Finally we were allowed on the plane and it took off. Eight hours later we landed and I got to see my mom! When she saw me, she gasped and I gave her a huge hug. She put a lei around my neck. A lei is a necklace made of real flowers. It was amazing and beautiful. We picked up my bags, then made our way to the ship. We found the den where we would sleep and I put my stuff away. We wanted to get an early start on our special day.

The next morning we woke up at six o'clock am. We started our day climbing Diamond Head Volcano. That might sound like fun to you, but just looking at the mountain made me exhausted! It was a very tiring climb, but once we got to the top it was all worth it. We could see the whole, lush green island!

Next we went snorkeling. We put on masks with snorkles and wore flippers on our feet. Mom and I laughed at each other, because we looked like alien space creatures. In a way we were, because the equipment let us enter another world under the water. I saw a lot of beautifully colored fish, and even got to pet a few.

This wonderful day ended with a luau. We watched as several people dug up a pig that had been cooking since 5:00 a.m. It was so cool—that was going to be our dinner! That pig was delicious. After dinner, men and women hula dancers put on a show. Women were cheering and whistling for the men dancers, and men were staring and drooling as they watched the women dance. The hula dancers even showed people how to do the hula. It was funny, like Comic View.

I have wanted to go to Hawaii ever since I was in second grade, so this was a dream come true. The thing that made this day most special, though, was spending time with my mom. We finally had a chance to bond, something we've needed ever since my dad left four years ago. I will treasure this memory and share it with my kids when I have some.

## Commentary

This student has a clear understanding of the purpose for writing and has addressed the writing prompt completely. Relevant details and vivid descriptions, major strengths in this paper, help the reader picture the events of the writer's special day. The writer's enthusiasm and excitement shine through the essay and are especially effective in drawing the reader into the narrative.

This narrative has a clear, consistent organizational structure. In addition, the student obviously demonstrates mastery of the conventions of English. The few errors that are present do not impede the reader's understanding of the narrative. A variety of sentence types is included, making the paper more interesting to read. The conclusion solidifies the essay, clearly summarizing the reasons that this day was the best thing that ever happened to the writer.

*(Go on to the next page.)*

The following sample represents a narrative that meets the criteria for a 3-point paper.

## Winning the Nationals

The best thing that ever happened to me was when my softball team won the Nationals in Springfield, Missouri. When I found out that I was going to go on a plane to Springfield, Missouri, my heart skipped a beat. I was so excited! When the day finally came, I had to wake up at 4:00 a.m. because I had to be at the airport by 6:00 a.m.

As we were aboarding the plane, I was saying goodbye to my parents. They couldn't come because they had to go to work. Finaly, I got on the plane and sat next to my friends. I asked them what it was like being on a plane, and they said that it's fun. Then I calmed down a little.

The planes engine started and I was nervous again. As the plane started to move, I could see my parents watching from the window. I wanted to go back, but it was too late. The plane was going faster and I could hear the engine getting louder and louder until finaly we took off. The ground faded as we got higher. Then all I could see was the clouds.

It was a long ride there, but I got through it. On the way there, I played cards, checkers, and ate some food. My friends really helped me get through the ride. I even forgot about the landing! When it was time to land, the flaps on the wings of the plane went up and we started to go down. We were going fast and were almost at the ground. All of a sudden, there was a huge thump, and we were on the ground. The brakes were squeeky, but they worked. We were in Springfield!

We got off the plane and went to the hotel. It was nice. We got ready for the first game. The game was tough, but we won. The second game was that day also. We won it, too. The next day we won two more games. Then it was time for the last game, the championship. I scored the winning run. Everybody jumped on me, and that was fun.

What made it so special to me was that this was the first time in my life that I have been out of California. It was the first time I've ever won the Nationals, meaning we are the top team in the whole nation. We got the best award anybody could ever have. We even got to be on the news about 10 times! That, my friends, was the best thing that ever happened to me!

## Commentary

This paper demonstrates a good understanding of the task, addressing all parts of the writing prompt. However, the writer has some difficulty maintaining a steady focus. The title suggests that winning the championship is the focus of the paper. Yet the first paragraph and most of the paper focus on the writer's travel experience. The concluding paragraph incorporates both the travel and playing experiences.

The events of the narrative are sufficiently developed, although the details could be richer. Limited descriptions, a shortage of sensory detail, and an inconsistent focus are the main reasons this paper scores three points instead of four.

The writer presents main ideas and related details in separate paragraphs, demonstrating a firm grasp of organizational structure. The writer also uses a variety of sentence types, making the essay more interesting. There are some errors in grammar, punctuation, capitalization, and spelling, but these do not interfere with the reader's understanding.

*(Go on to the next page.)*

The following sample represents a narrative that meets the criteria for a 2-point paper.

## Christmas Day

The best thing that ever happened to me was on Christmas day! My whole family comes together and we talk about what has been going on in our lives. I just played with my cousins. They are nice to me most of the time because they are so much older than me. That day my cousin Jewel who is around my age, we both went to the movies with the older kids. We had to put up a fight for it not a real one. They think that we are too young to go places with them. We went anyways and it was a lot of fun.

It happened when I was about twelve years old. A few years younger compared to my older cousins. I still have a couple around my age.

This took place in my grandmother's house. Her house is like no other in the world! Some call it strange I do, maybe it is her own style, anyways the reson that I say that my grandmother's house is strange is because right when you walk into her house there is Elvis posters and little Elvis toys, and even an Elvis clock too. So do you think that she likes Elvis presely? Uh-huh!

It was so special to me because it is a time where everyone no matter where you are come together and realized what you have is specail. So don't take your family for granded. I know I won't.

**Commentary**

The paper's first sentence presents the topic of this paper. However, the writing task has been addressed only superficially, demonstrating the writer's limited understanding of the purpose for writing. The writer lacks a clear focus. For example, one significant event—attending the movies with older relatives—is described in a muddled way. The writer then abandons the main idea and moves on to a discussion of his or her grandmother's house. There are few details, and descriptive language is limited.

While there is an effort to develop paragraphs, the overall organization needs improvement. Sentence structure is often weak; however, the student does use a limited variety of sentence types. The paper has several errors in spelling and punctuation that may interfere with the reader's understanding.

The following sample represents a narrative that meets the criteria for a 1-point paper.

The best thing that ever happened to me was when I was eight years old. I had spent the night over at my best freind's house. He had just got a rily cool dog and we played with him all night.

When I got home the next day, I askd my mom what would she think about getting a dog. She said she would think about it so for one month I kept asking for the dog, then it was chrismas when I woke up there was a little puppy laying on top of me.

Me and my freind marcus would always talk about one of the dogs being better. The thing that made it so specail was that i had my own dog to brag about.

**Commentary**

This paper briefly outlines two special events in the writer's life—spending the night with a friend and receiving a puppy. It is unclear which of these events is intended as the focus for this paper. The writer offers no title and there is no topic sentence in the first paragraph to make the paper's focus clear to the reader. The student attempts to address the writing prompt but succeeds only at a superficial level. The lack of details and description are typical of a paper scoring one point. Evidently, the writer did not understand the purpose of the writing assignment.

While the sentences are arranged in a logical order, there is no variety in sentence type. The paper has serious errors in spelling, grammar, punctuation, and capitalization that interfere with the reader's understanding.

# Sample How-to Papers

Before you begin the evaluation process, you may want to examine the following student papers and commentaries. The papers are examples of student writing at each level of the rubric. The commentaries provide explanations of why each paper received its rating.

The following sample represents a how-to paper that meets the criteria for a 4-point paper.

## Jumping on a Scooter

Scooters are very mobile, and you can do lots of tricks with them. If you don't know what a scooter is, it is a piece of metal aluminum with wheels on each side. On top of the front wheel there is a post with handlebars to hold on to. In this paper, I will teach you the process of actually jumping with the scooter.

To jump with the scooter, you must have the following essential items:
- a scooter* with the proper grip tape (so you don't fall)
- foam handlebars
- polyurethane wheels
- hand gloves (optional)
- protective knee pads, elbow pads, and forearm pads
- helmet
- tennis shoes
- comfortable clothing

*It must be a quality brand scooter. Try not to get a cheap, cheap, cheap scooter.

The items listed above are very important. The other important thing is the type of surface you will be riding and jumping on. The surface should be smooth with no potholes. Potholes can really hurt your wheels if they get stuck. Also, make sure there are no major rocks in the area.

Before you can jump with your scooter, you must learn to glide. First, put your hands on the handlebars. Don't grip too tightly or too loosely. You must be relaxed. Second, put one foot in the middle of the scooter. Bend your knees and shift your weight to your toes and push off with your other leg. Then, put that foot on the scooter behind your first foot. It does not matter if you use your right or your left foot to push off. You should be gliding now. If not, you must practice a little bit more.

Once you have perfected gliding, you are now ready to jump. When doing all tricks the first time, always start slowly. The jump you are about to do is called the Bunny Hop. Start gliding, then bend your knees. Grip the handlebars, then jump so that your knees touch your chest. At the same time, pull up the handlebars. You have just done the Bunny Hop. Start practicing, and when you've mastered this, try jumping over small objects and speed humps!

## Commentary

This student has a clear understanding of the purpose for writing and has thoroughly addressed the writing prompt. The how-to paper starts with a good title and introduction, stating the skill to be learned and describing what a scooter is. The student immediately lists the materials needed to perform the jump, along with extra information that could be helpful to the reader.

This how-to paper has a clear, consistent organizational structure, including an engaging introduction and conclusion. The student presents the task clearly and in a logical order, stating the steps in the process and using sequence words and paragraphs to delineate ideas. The writer offers clear, concise directions that are easy to follow. In addition, the student demonstrates mastery of the conventions of English. The few errors that are present do not impede the reader's understanding of the paper. This paper is an excellent example of a skillfully written how-to paper at the eighth-grade level.

*(Go on to the next page.)*

The following sample represents a how-to paper that meets the criteria for a 3-point paper.

### Fix Your Hair

One thing I know how to do well is putting my hair up in small sections with the use of tiny rubberbands. This hairstyle is very popular with young girls in this day and age. It's fast, easy, and fun! After one lesson, you will be a pro.

Very few materials are needed in order to complete this. You need small rubberbands by Goody. These usually come in a bag full of 200. You can purchase this item almost anywhere hair products are sold. You also need one regular-sized hair tie. These are also provided by Goody. These come in a bag of 8. You can also buy this where hair styling items are sold. Extra-hold hair spray is good, preferably Pantine Pro-V. The last thing you need is a separating comb.

Before you start, make sure you wash your hair thoroughly. Do not try to do this hairstyle when your hair is dry. It will not turn as well as if it is wet and brushed out nicely and neatly.

To start the hairstyle, first use the separating comb to part your hair down the middle of your head. Step 2, using the separating comb, separate your hair from right behind your left ear, all the way to your right ear. Tie up the extra hair in the back with the regular size hair tie so it won't get in the way. Next, use the separating comb to divide the sections from the part in the middle of your head. The sections should be about 1-inch square. Make sure to divide a section one at a time, then spray a little hair spray and use 1 rubberband to tie it up. Continue until you get to your ear. Repeat on the other side of your head. To complete the hair style, spray hair spray onto your hair so the hair style will stay nice and neat for a whole day. Have fun with your hair!

## Commentary

This writer presents an organized how-to paper that addresses all aspects of the writing prompt. The writer maintains her focus, organizes main ideas into paragraphs, and provides supporting details. The introductory paragraph is engaging and appealing to the writer's intended audience. The writer gives specific details about the materials that are needed for the task, and steps are sequenced logically.

The variety of sentence types is one of this paper's strengths. Its greatest weakness is its fourth paragraph, in which the writer describes the steps of the process. More elaborate directions would be helpful to readers who have never attempted this hairstyle.

There are some errors in grammar, punctuation, capitalization, and spelling, but these do not interfere with the reader's understanding of the task.

*(Go on to the next page.)*

The following sample represents a how-to paper that meets the criteria for a 2-point paper.

## Playing Soccer

You probably have heard of the sport soccer, but have you ever actually played soccer? The sport soccer is not very popular in America, but in other parts of the world such as, Europe, Central and South America. In fact in many countries, soccer is called futbol (football). I'm going to teach you how to play soccer, what you need to play soccer, and how to practice.

If you watch an experienced soccer team playing, you should take to notice that there are players that run, run, run, and they don't get the ball. This is because they need to be in the position that they could help another player if need be. They also are not wearing the clothes they wear to school or work either. They are probably wearing a uniform or practice uniform, and long socks. To play soccer you should wear loose clothes so that you can run easily, preferably shorts and a tee shirt. Wearing these clothes is still not enough, you are also going to need soccer equipment for your safety. You are going to need soccer cleats, shin guards, and also long soccer socks to cover the shin guards. Soccer cleats are special shoes made for playing soccer, the cleats you get should fit comfortably and not be too loose and not too tight either. They also need to have no toe cleat or spike on the toe for the safety of you and your opponent, because the toe cleat could cause you to trip, or cause injury your opponent when you're trying to get the ball. Shin guards are a type of soccer equipment that protects your shins, because if you're playing then you can get accidentally kicked in the shins. The socks you get should be your size and fit comfortably. When you are putting on your socks remember to put them over the shin guards so the shin guards don't move while you are running or you can get hurt. Also when you by your equipment make sure that it is not too heavy and going to weigh you down. So when getting ready to practice you put on your uniform, shin guards, soccer socks, and then your soccer cleats.

Now that you know what to wear, you need is to your size soccer ball. The soccer balls com in sizes such as, size three for 4-8 year olds, size four for 8-12 year olds, and size five for 12 year olds and up. With eight and twelve year olds they need the ball to be the size for what age they are when they start the season. The ball also needs to be properly inflated. To see how inflated the ball is you put the ball against your chest and push lightly on the same square, and it should go in about 1/4th an inch it's properly inflated.

Now that you have all the equipment all you need is a soccer field to practice on and another person to help you with practicing. To practice you should start out with stretching such as flamingos, or keeping your legs straight and trying to touch the grass, and running some laps. Next try passing with each other and then kicking hard into an area (shooting), and other things such as dribbling, kicking/shooting. So, now you know most of the basics of soccer.

## Commentary

This paper demonstrates earnest effort, familiarity with the topic, and some understanding of the purpose for writing. The first paragraph promises the reader that the writer will discuss "…how to play soccer, what you need to play soccer, and how to practice." Had the subsequent paragraphs fulfilled the writer's promise, they should have followed a different sequence. However, that point is irrelevant given that the writer provides few details regarding how to practice or play soccer.

The overall organization of the paper is adequate, although for the most part, the conclusion is absent. There are errors in the conventions of the English language that may make reading difficult.

*(Go on to the next page.)*

The following sample represents a how-to paper that meets the criteria for a 1-point paper.

### Computers

I am going to explain to you how to use a computer. I like playing games, going on the Internet and goint to programs, but a computer can do much more, but first before I tell you how to use a computer I will tell you what a computer is. A computer is a mechanic item that lets you go on the Internet, talk with people, go on the web, download stuff, go into programs, and can let you play games.

O.K. now I will tell you the steps you use for using a computer. First buy a computer. second hook up your computer in your house and then turn on your computer and start enstal programs, when you first turn on the computer the computer will gide you to programs, tells you how to use the keybord and mouse, and lets you download program you want. Then when you are done download a Internet program so you can go on the Internet and start going on web sites, make your own email address and start downloading stuff. Well you can still do allot of stuff with out going on the Internet. For the busnes people you can make data tables, type, print, draw and listen to music. For kids you can record your voice, play games, paint write to your girlfriend, take picture of you doggies, and other kinds of stuff kids do.

There are much more to a computer than playing games so please buy a computer.

## Commentary

This student attempts to address the writing prompt; however, he or she chose an inappropriate topic for a how-to paper. While the student uses sequence words and orders the basic steps in the process, the topic is too complex for the student to explain adequately. Thus, the reader is left unable to complete the steps and use a computer.

While the writer does give a sense of enthusiasm for the task, he or she has little understanding of the purpose of the writing assignment. The paper lacks a strong introduction and conclusion, directions are muddled, and sentence structures are weak. The paper has a number of serious errors in spelling, punctuation, and grammar that impede the reader's understanding.

# Sample Persuasive Papers

Before you begin the evaluation process, you may want to examine the following student papers and commentaries. The papers are examples of student writing at each level of the rubric. The commentaries provide explanations of why each paper received its rating.

The following sample represents a persuasive movie review that meets the criteria for a 4-point paper.

### Remember the Titans

A wonderful film to see is called <u>Remember the Titans</u>. It is a must-see film. I love the way the film mixes the topics of segregation and integration with football. It gives everyone who sees the film something to think about.

A coach from out of town moves to a southern community of blacks and whites. This new coach, Coach Boone, is a young black man who is there to try-out as the new coach for high school. He gets the job and the black boys in high school are extremely excited! Not everyone is excited, though, as you'll find out when Coach Boone has his first team meeting.

Coach Boone is determined to make sure that the team is fully integrated. When they went to Ghettysberg camp, Coach Boone made sure that no one of the same race would room together. He made the boys do three-a-day practices until all of the boys, black or white, got on the same social level. There is a scene where the boys are doing a practice and a young black boy and white boy start to associate. They show the rest of the team it's okay to be friends, even if your skin color is the opposite of mine. The next day the lunch hall was filled with laughter from both races. They were all talking, together.

When you see the movie, you'll find out about all the problems Coach Boone and the team faced, even though they all got along. This movie will touch your very soul, bring a smile to your lips, and a tear to your eye. This is why it is a must-see movie.

## Commentary

Clearly, this writer enjoyed seeing *Remember the Titans*. The writer tells us in the first paragraph that the movie's themes of segregation, integration, and football make this a movie worth seeing.

The writer addresses all parts of the writing task, showing a clear understanding of the purpose for writing. This is a well-developed review, in which the writer summarizes the film's highlights without disclosing too many details. The writer seems to have a sense of what information is important and what will appeal to his or her audience.

The organizational structure of the essay is well developed and logical, with strong opening and closing paragraphs. The writer employs a variety of sentence types to keep the review interesting and follows the conventions of English. Existing errors are few and do not interfere with comprehension.

*(Go on to the next page.)*

The following sample represents a persuasive movie review that meets the criteria for a 3-point paper.

## Pearl Harbor

The best movie I have seen recently is <u>Pearl Harbor</u>. I saw it on the 4th of July. It was a sad story about love, friendship, and family. The movie was so realistic, it was like I was really there.

<u>Pearl Harbor</u> is diffrent from other movies. It is nothing like I have seen before. I almost cried during the movie. Also, nobody has done a historic movie since <u>Titanic</u>. To me, <u>Pearl Harbor</u> was better and more tragic than <u>Titanic</u>.

Some movies are loved because they are funny, but I like this movie because it teaches everyone a lesson. It also lets us observe on what happened on that historic day. At the end of the movie, everyone in the movie is sad. The two main characters fall in love, and they remember their friends who had died in the war.

I think other people should see this movie so they can share my experiences. Although it was sad, <u>Pearl Harbor</u> was a good movie.

**Commentary**

This movie review addresses all parts of the writing task and shows a general understanding of purpose. It is adequately developed, with a mainly consistent point of view. While the student includes reasons for seeing the movie, he or she does not elaborate upon them. The absence of meaningful supporting details is this review's greatest weakness.

The student demonstrates an understanding of organizational structure and includes a variety of sentence types. There are some errors in grammar and spelling, but none that hampers understanding.

---

The following sample represents a persuasive movie review that meets the criteria for a 2-point paper.

## The Others

The best movie I have seen recently is The Others. The Others is the best movie to me because there is a twist ending and it is scarey through the whole movie.

What makes this movie different from others is it just scared me more than some of the other movies I have seen for a long time. I really liked this movie because of the ending.

I think others should see this movie because it is a scarey movie. Everybody who likes scarey movies should go see it because I really like the acting in the movie.

**Commentary**

The writer addresses some parts of the writing task but demonstrates little understanding of the purpose for writing. The first mention of the writer's desire for others to see this movie doesn't come until the last paragraph.

The writer fails to state the reasons that make the movie worth seeing in a clear and logical manner. Consequently, the reader must sift through the content to learn that the movie's surprise ending, frightening content, and acting are its positive features.

The review is minimally developed. It offers few details and little content to enable the reader to visualize the movie. There are also several errors in grammar, spelling, and punctuation that may interfere with a reader's understanding.

*(Go on to the next page.)*

The following sample represents a persuasive movie review that meets the criteria for a 1-point paper.

## The Outsiders

the outsidrs is a great movie. It's about this boy named Ponyboy who lost his mom and dad years ago now he lives with his brothers Sodapopand Darrie. Soon he stumbles into a hole lot of bad things with to Socs.becaues he and Jonny flirted with their X girl freinds Cherry and Marcia .After it all ends Pony boy gets a old letter from his dead freind Jonny befor he died it spoke of a poem that Ponyboy could not under stand it ment stay gold Stevie Wounder sang a song called stay gold for this classic movie and Emilio Estives and Tom Cruz were also in volved in this movie by playing roles like freinds of the main charter and S.E. Hinton the writer of this story was offered he part as a nures. All in all the outsiders a great movie even though it has violence and cussing please step outside and see this movie!!

## Commentary

This student addresses one part of the writing task—identifying a favorite movie. However, the student offers no reasons why someone might want to see the movie. The absence of persuasive reasons demonstrates that the writer had little or no understanding of the purpose for writing.

The review summarizes the movie's plot but lacks a persuasive focus. The writer fails to establish main ideas and organize them in any sensible way. Errors in grammar, spelling, and punctuation overwhelm this paper, making it difficult for the reader to understand. This writer needs considerable guidance if he or she is to write a truly persuasive movie review.

# Proofreading Marks

Use the following symbols to help make proofreading faster.

| Mark | Meaning | Example |
|------|---------|---------|
| ⬭ | spell correctly | I (liek) dogs. |
| ⊙ | add period | They are my favorite kind of pet⊙ |
| ? | add question mark | Are you lucky enough to have a dog? |
| ≡ | capitalize | My dog's name is scooter. |
| ℛ | take out | He is a great companion for me and my m~~y~~ family. |
| ∧ | add | We got Scooter when ^he was eight weeks old. |
| / | make lower case | My Ʉncle came over to take a look at him. |
| ∿ | trade places | He watched the puppy run⁀in⁀around⁀circles. |
| ⋀, | add comma | "Jack‿that dog is a real scooter!" he told me. |
| ⱽ ⱽ | add quotation marks | ⱽScooter! That's the perfect name!ⱽI said. |
| ¶ | indent paragraph | ¶ Scooter is my best friend in the whole world. He is not only happy and loving but also the smartest dog in the world. Every morning at six o'clock, he jumps on my bed and wakes me with a bark. Then he brings me my toothbrush. |

# The Writing Process

In writing, you can use a plan to help you think of ideas and then write about them. This plan is called a *writing process*. Here are the steps of the writing process.

## Step 1: Prewriting

Think about why you are writing. What is your purpose, or goal? Who are you writing for?

Choose a topic, or something to write about. Make notes. Organize your notes in a way that makes sense.

## Step 2: Drafting

Use your ideas and notes from the first step to begin writing.

## Step 3: Revising

Read your draft. Is the purpose of your paper clear?

Share your writing with someone else. Talk about what is good about your paper and what could make it better.

## Step 4: Proofreading

Correct any mistakes you find in spelling, grammar, punctuation, and capitalization.

## Step 5: Publishing

Make a clean copy of your paper.

Share your paper with others.

### Moving Back and Forth

All together, there are five steps in the writing process. However, as you write, you may move back and forth through the steps several times before you reach your writing goal.

You may return to your draft many times to make it better. Go back and forth often. The extra steps will improve your writing and help you publish your best work.

# Types of Writing

In this book you will read examples of different kinds of writing. Then you will practice your own writing skills. You will write to…

- **Tell a Story**

  A story is also called a narrative. A narrative has…
  - one or more characters.
  - a setting, or place and time for the story to happen.
  - a plot that includes a problem that is solved step by step.

- **Tell About a Part of Your Life**

  An autobiographical sketch tells about part of your life. It includes…
  - important events that happened to you.
  - details that describe the events that happened.

- **Describe Someone or Something**

  When you describe something or someone, you share details. Details can be…
  - facts.
  - information that comes from using your senses of hearing, sight, smell, touch, and taste.
  - dialogue, or words that people say.
  - thoughts and feelings.

- **Explain How to Do Something**

  When you explain how to do something, you talk about…
  - the materials someone needs.
  - the steps someone should follow in order.
  - important details.

- **Show How Two Things, Places, or People Are Alike and Different**

  To explain how two things are alike and different, you…
  - use reference materials to find information on a topic.
  - organize main ideas about the topic to show how two things are alike.
  - organize main ideas about the topic to show how two things are different.
  - include important details.

# Types of Writing, page 2

- **Share Information in a Short Report**

  To write a good report, you...
  - choose a specific topic.
  - decide what you would like to learn about your topic.
  - use reference materials to collect information about your topic.
  - use facts, not opinions.

- **Convince Someone**

  When you write persuasively, you...
  - share your opinion or position on a topic.
  - try to make someone agree with you.
  - try to convince someone to do something.

# A Model Paper

## A Personal Narrative

### Pride or Prejudice?

All kids need friends, especially new kids at Jordan Middle School. My name is Jane Austen Street and I, unfortunately, am one of those new kids. A lot of new kids don't have any trouble fitting in. They make friends fast. But I'm not one of them. I don't talk about myself in the first person. I've never had an adventure in baby-sitting. I don't wear designer clothes. And, I can never think of just the right thing to say when some kid at school makes me a target of a smart remark. Not that I want to say something smart, you understand. I'm not interested in working hard to be like everybody else. I want to be me, but it takes time. And kids like Madison James just don't get it.

The other day, for example, I wore my overalls to school. I know overalls aren't for everybody, but I like them. Anyway, between classes Madison yells at me in the hall. I'm standing in front of the principal and *every* eighth-grader at Jordan Middle School when I hear, "Hey, Farmer Street, where's your cow?" I knew I was as red as a late summer tomato because I could feel my face burning. I didn't say anything. Instead, I smiled a pathetic smile and slipped away like I didn't exist.

For the moment, Madison James is my living nightmare. She's the eyelash on my contact. She's the dried blob in my hair gel. She's the...the...well, you get the idea. Ever since I moved across town to Jordan Middle School, Madison has been a pain in my side.

First thing every morning, I look at Madison. She's in Ms. Mitchell's first-period English class just like me. Madison is also the last person I see every day. That's because she and I are in gym last period. She's everywhere I am and everywhere I look. And, she's everything I'm not and everything I don't want to be. She looks like she just stepped out of a magazine. You know what I mean. She's shiny and glossy and, well, together. She's popular and she knows it. She doesn't talk to me unless she has something nasty to say. And she doesn't look at me without squinting. Her eyes practically disappear into hateful lines across her face.

I wasn't surprised when Madison's attention turned to my name. In fact, I was surprised it hadn't happened sooner. Ms. Mitchell started it when she passed out copies of *Pride and Prejudice.* The writer's name is the same as mine—Jane Austen. Obviously, that's not my fault. But as soon as Madison heard the name, she blurted, "Jane Austen? That's your name."

I rolled my eyes, hoping the rest of the class would think that Madison's observation was too obvious, if you know what I mean. "She's my mother's favorite author," I answered casually, pretending that the matter wasn't worth discussing. What I wasn't willing to say was that I like Jane Austen, too. And, so far anyway, *Pride and Prejudice* is my all-time favorite book. I've read it five times already. But there are some things even I know it's smarter to keep to yourself when you're in eighth grade.

Ms. Mitchell explained that Jane Austen lived more than 200 years ago. Madison swung her head around, zeroing in on me like an angry bee with a stinger. "Your mother named you after a dead writer?" A few people in my class snickered. The others seemed bored.

"I'm named after a dead writer. You're named after a dead president. But you only got his last name." More people seemed to be paying attention this time. I heard more laughter. So did Madison, who looked, probably for the first time in her life, unsure of herself. She turned around without saying anything.

When I saw Madison's reaction, I felt ashamed. As much as I hated being new and not fitting in right away, I also hated acting like this. My smart remark made me no different than Madison. But I didn't have time to think about it. Ms. Mitchell was giving class assignments.

"I want you to read this book with a partner," Ms. Mitchell said. "You have one week. Then, you and your partner will present a short report to the class on a topic that I'll give you today. Madison and Jane," she smiled, looking directly at us, "I want you two to report on what we can learn from the main characters in *Pride and Prejudice*."

When Ms. Mitchell finished giving assignments, Madison and I took our pass and went to the library. We found a table in the back. Neither of us said anything at first. Then Madison said, "So what's this book about? You must know if you're named after the author."

"Well," I said slowly, "it's about two people who get the wrong idea about each other. One character, Mr. Darcy, is shy. He finds it hard talking to people he doesn't know. Because Mr. Darcy never says anything, Elizabeth Bennet, the other character, thinks he's proud, or stuck up. When Mr. Darcy realizes that Elizabeth has made up her mind about him without getting to know him first, he decides she's prejudiced."

Madison looked at me but didn't say anything right away. Then she smiled a little smile. "So they're wrong about each other," she said.

"Sort of. I mean, Mr. Darcy *is* a snob and Elizabeth *does* judge people too quickly. But their ideas about each other are all wrong. It takes them a while to see each other as they really are." I started feeling nervous as Madison's smile grew larger.

"You mean like us?" she asked. "You acted like you didn't like me from the start. Like you didn't like the way I dress or something."

"That's not it really. You squint at me all the time. And you never stop teasing me," I said.

"Squinting? Oh, that. My mother says that, too. I'm nearsighted, and I don't like to wear my glasses. And my eyes water if I wear contacts. And teasing? I do that with all of my friends. That means I like you."

This time, I was smiling. "Oh, I get it. Then do you think you could like me a little less?"

We both laughed.

"I think I might like reading this book after all," said Madison, squinting at me. "Sounds like the author knows a lot about people."

Suddenly, it hit me. Madison could turn out to be a friend after all.

# Respond to the Model Paper

| **Directions** | Write your answers to the following questions or directions. |

1.  How does Jane describe herself? How does she describe Madison?

    _____

    _____

    _____

2.  How did Jane and Madison get wrong ideas about each other?

    _____

    _____

    _____

3.  Write a paragraph to summarize the story. Use these questions to help you write your summary:

    • What is Jane's problem at Jordan Middle School?
    • Why does Jane dislike Madison?
    • How is Jane's problem solved?

    _____

    _____

    _____

    _____

    _____

    _____

    _____

    _____

    _____

    _____

    _____

    _____

    _____

# Analyze the Model Paper

 **Directions** ➤ Read "Pride or Prejudice?" again. As you read, think about how the writer wrote the story. Write your answers to the following questions or directions.

1.  How do you know that this is a personal narrative?

    _____

    _____

    _____

2.  Read the first paragraph again. What problem does the writer present in this paragraph?

    _____

    _____

    _____

3.  In the third paragraph, the writer uses several metaphors. Why do you think the writer used this technique to describe Madison? Name a technique the writer uses to describe herself.

    _____

    _____

    _____

4.  Why do you think the writer included the novel *Pride and Prejudice* in this story? In other words, what purpose does the novel serve other than to explain how Jane got her name?

    _____

    _____

    _____

    _____

    _____

Name _____   Date _____

# Writing Assignment

 **Directions** Think about someone you know who is special to you. Write a personal narrative about this person. Use examples and details to show why this person is special. Use this writing plan to help you write.

## Writing Plan

Who is the person you will write about?

Tell what makes this person special to you.

Give examples to show why this person is special.

# First Draft

> ## Tips for Writing a Personal Narrative:
> - Write from your point of view. Use the words *I* and *my* to show your readers that this is your story.
> - Think about what you want to tell your reader.
> - Organize your ideas into a beginning, middle, and end.
> - Write an interesting introduction that "grabs" your readers.
> - Write an ending for your story. Write it from your point of view.

## First Draft

**Directions** ▷ Use your writing plan as a guide for writing your first draft of a *Personal Narrative.*

_____

_____

_____

_____

_____

_____

_____

_____

_____

_____

_____

_____

*(Continue on your own paper.)*

# Revise the Draft

Use the chart below to help you revise your draft. Check *Yes* or *No* to answer each question in the chart. If you answer *No*, make notes to remind yourself how you can revise, or change, your writing to improve it.

| Question | Yes ✔ | No ✔ | If the answer is no, what will you do to improve your writing? |
|---|---|---|---|
| Does your story describe someone special to you? | | | |
| Do you use specific examples to explain why this person is special? | | | |
| Do you describe events in the order they happened? | | | |
| Do you include important details? | | | |
| Does your conclusion summarize your story in a new way? | | | |
| Do you tell your story from your point of view? | | | |
| Have you corrected mistakes in spelling, grammar, and punctuation? | | | |

**Directions** ⟩ Use the notes in your chart and writing plan to revise your draft.

# Writing Report Card

**Directions** ► Read your revised draft again or ask someone else to read it. Have the person who reads your paper complete the following Report Card. Revise your paper until you have no less than a Very Good Score for each item.

Title of paper: _____

Purpose of paper: ___This paper is a personal narrative. It talks about someone who is special to me.___

Person who scores the paper: _____

| Score | Writing Goals |
|---|---|
| | Is the story told from a first-person point of view? |
| | Does the story have a strong beginning, or introduction? |
| | Does the story include specific examples to explain why the person in the story is special? |
| | Are there details to support each example? |
| | Do events in the story happen in order? |
| | Are there different kinds of sentences, such as questions, dialogue, and descriptions, that help make the story interesting? |
| | Does the story have a strong ending, or conclusion? |
| | Are the story's grammar, spelling, and punctuation correct? |

☺ Excellent Score        ☆ Very Good Score        + Good Score

✔ Acceptable Score        — Needs Improvement

# A Model Paper

## An Autobiographical Sketch

## *A Change of Heart*

The bus ride from Dallas was the first sign that I wouldn't like Texas. The rocking bus made me sick to my stomach. Plus, the farther I traveled from the airport, the more depressed I felt. I leaned my head against the bus's grimy glass window and watched Texas roll by. The city changed into small towns, which then dissolved into endless flat, brown, dusty fields. I had imagined places like this while I was reading *The Martian Chronicles*. This was Mars, wasn't it? Where were the video arcades, the all-night pizza parlors, the neon lights, and the traffic? Modern civilization had disappeared, and I knew I hated Texas!

In a way, this trip started last summer. That was when I met Tyrone at a computer camp in upstate New York. We hit it off from the start, so when he invited me to visit him the next summer, I didn't say no right away. I didn't say yes either, you understand. I had never been outside New York before, and Texas seemed a million miles away. But both my mom and dad thought Tyrone's idea was great. They were all for it. In fact, their exact words were, "The experience will be good for you." At the time, I had no idea what they meant.

Tyrone and his mom met me at the bus depot in San Angelo. I was relieved to see them, but not relieved to learn we still had thirty miles to go in the Peterson's old pickup truck.

Mrs. Peterson drove the truck down roads dotted with potholes. My head bobbed up and down so hard that I knew if I tried to speak, I'd bite my tongue in half. So I watched silently as the scenery changed from dusty to dustier. Eventually, we turned down a hidden road and into a lane with a barred gate. Tyrone jumped out to open the gate and closed it again after Mrs. Peterson drove through. "We've got lots of animals," he said, pointing proudly to a small herd of horses.

The truck bumped down a deeply rutted track. The truck stopped outside what looked like a soda can on wheels. "Where are we?" I asked Tyrone. He opened the door on the can and announced proudly, "We're home. Come on in."

Tyrone's dad met us at the door. He had dinner ready, and although I didn't recognize the smell, I was starving. Somewhere near the first bite, my eyes watered and I couldn't catch my breath. Tyrone smacked my back, making me spit a mouthful of King Ranch Chicken back on my plate. "This is really good," I said to Mr. Peterson through my tears. The Petersons laughed while I pushed everything that looked like a chili to the edge of my plate.

While I recovered from my near-death experience, Tyrone unpacked for me. It was late and I was worn out. Tyrone could see that I was tired. "I'll wake you up early so we can search for arrowheads before it gets too hot. Sound okay to you?" I nodded and then the lights went out.

The trailer's rocking woke me. Thunder boomed and lightning flashed. In one flash, I looked over at Tyrone—he was sleeping soundly in his bed. Was the rocking of the trailer normal, or should I wake him up to tell him we might wind up in Oz any minute? "New York, I miss you. Texas, I hate you." Those were my last thoughts before I finally fell back into an exhausted sleep.

Early the next morning, Tyrone and I went outside. The sun was already bright, and the sky was a fresh-washed brilliant blue. I could see clean lines and shapes for miles in every direction. Then I noticed something else. "Tyrone, I don't think I've ever heard so much quiet before." He understood and laughed.

Mrs. Peterson called from the trailer, "Boys, watch out for snakes! Breakfast is almost ready, so come in and wash your hands!"

"Snakes?" I said to Tyrone, stopping in my tracks.

"Yesssssss," he said in a scary voice, "ssssssnakessss. Rattlessssnaakessssss."

"I hate Texas," I said very quietly under my breath.

After breakfast, we set off with a packed lunch and a hoe to kill any rattlesnakes we might see. I wasn't too happy about the rattlesnake part, but Tyrone said that we might find Indian arrowheads after the rain.

"What kind of Indians were around here?" I asked.

"Lots of different tribes over thousands of years. Comanche, Lipan, Anasazi. We might find something really old."

We reached a gully where Tyrone showed me what flint, the kind of rock the Indians used to chip arrowheads, looked like. He told me, "Head uphill into the sun. Scan the ground and look for anything that catches the light in an unusual way. If you see a rock that looks like it's been worked, pick it up and call me over. If you see or hear a snake, stand still, and call me over."

"Don't worry. I will." At first, it was hard to see so much at once, but after a while, I could spot pieces of flint and chips from arrowheads. By then, even the fear of stepping on a snake had moved to the back of my mind. Hours passed as Tyrone and I moved slowly, inching our way up another bluff. Finally, there it was, lying half in and half out of the sandy ground. I had the feeling that I had been looking at it for several seconds without seeing it. If I had discovered an Egyptian tomb, I couldn't have been more stunned.

"Tyrone, I found one. I found an arrowhead. Wow, a big one."

"Man, that's not just an arrowhead, that's a spear point!"

We started digging. The spearhead was about eight inches long and perfectly formed out of a white translucent flint.

"Wow, let's take it to dad. I bet he'll know what it is. Or, maybe we can go into San Angelo tomorrow to visit the old fort. There are experts there who know all about Indian artifacts. You can see the Buffalo Soldier exhibit there, too. The Buffalo Soldiers were black soldiers stationed at the fort in the late 1800s. The Comanches gave them the name of Buffalo as a sign of respect because the soldiers were brave."

As we started hiking back to the trailer, I cradled the spear point carefully. The silent beauty of the land struck me as I looked out on a landscape that had been unchanged for perhaps thousands of years. I felt small but important at the same time. There were no crowds of people to blend into, no haze smearing the landscape, no blaring radios or horns. Only me. Only this incredibly bright, quiet, bold land. Maybe Texas wasn't so bad after all.

# Respond to the Model Paper

**Directions** ▷ Write your answers to the following questions or directions.

1.  In an autobiographical sketch, a writer talks about something important that happened to him or her. What important thing happened to this writer?

    _____

    _____

    _____

2.  How would you describe the setting for this story?

    _____

    _____

    _____

3.  What is the first clue the writer gives you to explain that a change of heart might be happening?

    _____

    _____

    _____

4.  Write a paragraph to summarize the story. Use these questions to help you write your summary:

    • What are the main ideas in this story?
    • What happens first? Second? Third?
    • How does the story end?

    _____

    _____

    _____

    _____

    _____

    _____

    _____

# Analyze the Model Paper

 **Directions** ▷ Read "A Change of Heart" again. As you read, think about how the writer wrote the story. Answer the following questions.

1.  This story has an interesting beginning. In the first paragraph, a gloomy mood, or feeling, is created immediately. Then, in the second paragraph, the mood changes. How did the writer create these changing moods?

    _____

    _____

    _____

2.  Read the second paragraph again. How does the writer suggest that the main character faces unusual challenges?

    _____

    _____

    _____

3.  What does the writer use in the ninth paragraph to shift the mood of the story?

    _____

    _____

    _____

4.  How does the writer use the last paragraph to convince you that the main character has had a change of heart?

    _____

    _____

    _____

    _____

    _____

    _____

    _____

Name _____     Date _____

# Writing Assignment

 **Directions** ▷ Write an autobiographical sketch about something important that happened to you. Write about something you remember well. Use this writing plan to help you write.

## Writing Plan

**What important thing happened to you?**

**What happened first? How will you describe it?**

**What happened second? How will you describe it?**

**What happened last? How will you describe it?**

# First Draft

> ## Tips for Writing an Autobiographical Sketch:
> ● Write about something important that happened to you.
> ● Write about something you remember well.
> ● Give details that help explain your experience.
> ● Describe events in the order that they happened.

## First Draft

**Directions** ⟩ Use your writing plan as a guide for writing your first draft of an *Autobiographical Sketch.*

_____

_____

_____

_____

_____

_____

_____

_____

_____

_____

_____

_____

*(Continue on your own paper.)*

# Revise the Draft

**Directions** ⟩ Use the chart below to help you revise your draft. Check *Yes* or *No* to answer each question in the chart. If you answer *No*, make notes to remind yourself how you can revise, or change, your writing to improve it.

| Question | Yes ✔ | No ✔ | If the answer is no, what will you do to improve your writing? |
|---|---|---|---|
| Does your autobiographical sketch describe something important that happened to you? | | | |
| Does your story have a clear setting? | | | |
| Do you include important characters in your story? | | | |
| Do you describe events in the order they happen? | | | |
| Do you use specific details to help you tell your story? | | | |
| Have you corrected mistakes in spelling, grammar, and punctuation? | | | |

**Directions** ⟩ Use the notes in your chart and writing plan to revise your draft.

# Writing Report Card

**Directions** Read your revised draft again or ask someone else to read it. Have the person who reads your paper complete the following Report Card. Revise your paper until you have no less than a Very Good Score for each item.

Title of paper: _____

Purpose of paper: _____ This paper is an autobiographical sketch. It describes

something important that happened in my life. _____

Person who scores the paper: _____

| Score | Writing Goals |
|---|---|
| | Is this story an example of an autobiographical sketch? |
| | Is the setting described in detail? |
| | Does the writer use important characters to help tell the story? |
| | Does the writer describe specific events? |
| | Does the writer use important details to help explain events? |
| | Does the writer describe events in the order they happen? |
| | Does the writer convince you that this experience was important to him or her? |
| | Are the story's grammar, spelling, and punctuation correct? |

☺ Excellent Score        ☆ Very Good Score        + Good Score

✔ Acceptable Score        — Needs Improvement

# A Model Paper

## A Descriptive Story

## *Lost!*

The day hadn't started the way Yuki thought it would. She woke feeling tired and grumpy, not the best frame of mind for a ten-mile hike to Blue Hole with the Explorers Club. Then, when she met her best friend, Jada, at the start of the hike, they quarreled about something stupid. Blue Hole was a fantastic place to swim, but Yuki couldn't get excited about walking for hours through thick woods. She struggled to keep up with the others, bringing up the rear of a snaking line of ten other kids led by the club leader, Ms. Reeves.

It was mid-morning when the group stopped for its first water break. Jada sat with some other friends, ignoring Yuki. Yuki felt snubbed and was even more out of sorts. When the group reassembled to resume the hike, Yuki deliberately stayed near the back. "I know this trail," she thought to herself. "I'll take a longer rest and then catch up later." When the last hiker was out of sight, Yuki stretched out at the base of a pine tree. Fingers of sunlight stretched sideways through tree branches to warm her face. Yuki yawned, scrunched down into the roots of the tree, and fell into a deep sleep.

A woodpecker tapped on a branch above Yuki's head, waking her instantly. For a moment, she didn't know where she was. Then Yuki's dry and furry mouth told her that she had slept too long. "What have I done?" Yuki leaped up and started running down the trail. "I've got to catch up!" she thought desperately. Branches and vines clawed and slapped at her as she jogged down the path. Some distance later, Yuki was breathless and felt a vicious thirst. She stopped, holding her aching side with one hand and using the other to fumble through her pack, searching for her half-full water bottle. Despite knowing that she should save some for later, Yuki couldn't stop drinking once the cool water began to trickle over her cracked lips and parched tongue. She stopped drinking when the bottle was dry.

It was then that she felt the raging fire on her face that would undoubtedly cause her skin to blister and peel. The sun must have moved above the trees and baked her while she slept. That meant that she had slept far longer than she had intended. Suddenly, she noticed how long the shadows were. "It must be at least the middle of the afternoon," she thought to herself. The path she was following narrowed to a dark point. "This is a deer trail, not the way to Blue Hole." Fear bubbled up from her belly as she realized her mistake. "I don't know where I am," she whispered to the woods.

Yuki's tears made the forest dip and shimmer, turning it into a runny watercolor of greens and blues. Slowly she tried to retrace her steps, following the slender deer trail. "I have to get back to the place where I slept," she thought desperately. She walked a while but couldn't find her "sleeping tree." Surely by now, Ms. Reeves and the group had come to look for her. Chances were they'd find her before dark. But if they didn't, she'd have to spend the night in the woods.

"Heeelllp! Help me!" yelled Yuki in her panic. "I'm here. Please, I'm over here!"

The woods swallowed her screams, and every other sound, too. There were no buzzing insects, no chirping birds, no scurrying squirrels. She'd never heard such silence before. She'd never felt so alone.

Slowly, a red bird began a sweet song whose notes fell from the tree branches like drops of rain. Joining in, a blue jay scolded, then a bee buzzed by, a squirrel chattered, and a crow cawed. At last, the forest symphony was playing again, and Yuki felt calmer.

She had to get a grip on herself. She couldn't let fear lead her into any more stupid decisions. "Think. Use your head," she said to herself, remembering her grandmother's constant warning to think before acting. "Be an actor, not a reactor," she used to say. There was something else her grandmother used to say. Being positive changes bad luck into good luck. So far today, Yuki thought glumly, she had forgotten everything her grandmother had taught her. Now seemed like a good time to start remembering.

She sat down and ate the last of a leftover breakfast bar. She worked hard to ignore her thirst. She focused instead on trying to determine where she was and from which direction she had come. Then she remembered the reason she had chosen the pine tree where she had slept. It was the tallest tree around, and its top branches were bald.

Yuki drew a line of forest litter to mark her path as she left the trail to find the nearest outcropping of rocks overlooking the forest. She scanned the forest top, turning in a slow circle. She saw no bald trees peeking above the canopy. She turned again, making herself look calmly at every detail. About a half-mile away, she saw a tall evergreen tree with a bald top crowning thick green limbs. Yuki used her eyes to draw an imaginary line between her sleeping tree and the top of a tree close to the trail. She abandoned the outcrop, heading toward the tree. When she reached it, she stopped and left the trail to scan the woods from another outcropping. There, she took another sighting, drew another imaginary line, and jumped back on the trail. At last, she reached her sleeping tree. Her footprints dented the ground by the rock, and the trail the others had followed that morning was nearby.

There was a chance the kids in the Explorers Club had already come back this way. Yuki got down on her hands and knees, searching the trail for tracks. Small jagged rocks and woody acorns hid beneath dead leaves covering the trail. They punched Yuki's palms and knees as she moved slowly over the ground. Yuki felt the pain but kept moving. The only footprints she found went toward Blue Hole. No one had returned, but that was good news. All she had to do now was wait. She knew she would be in trouble with Ms. Reeves and the club, but she knew that she deserved to be. She also knew that she could have been in much worse trouble if she hadn't started acting instead of reacting. Relief left Yuki almost lighthearted. She went back to the sleeping tree, where she sat in late-afternoon darkness thinking positive thoughts.

Shortly before the sun said goodnight, Yuki heard the welcome sound of voices. Her grandmother was right again.

# Respond to the Model Paper

**Directions** ⟩ Write your answers to the following questions or directions.

1. Describe the setting where Yuki was hiking.

   _____

   _____

   _____

2. What were Yuki's reasons for staying behind?

   _____

   _____

   _____

3. How did Yuki get lost?

   _____

   _____

   _____

4. Write a paragraph to summarize the story. Use these questions to help you write your summary:

   • What are the main ideas of the story?
   • What happens first? Second? Third?
   • How does the story end?

   _____

   _____

   _____

   _____

   _____

   _____

   _____

   _____

   _____

# Analyze the Model Paper

 **Directions** ⟩ Read "Lost!" again. As you read, think about how the writer achieved his or her purpose for writing. Write your answers to the following questions or directions.

1.  Read the second paragraph again. On another piece of paper, draw a picture of Yuki as you see her at the end of this paragraph.

2.  The writer uses some interesting descriptions, such as *vicious thirst* and *raging fire.* Why are these descriptions important to the story?

    _____

    _____

    _____

    _____

    _____

3.  Read the fifth paragraph again. What metaphor does the writer use to describe what the forest looks like to Yuki? Write another metaphor to describe the forest the way Yuki sees it at this moment in the story.

    _____

    _____

    _____

    _____

    _____

4.  Write a new paragraph to change the story's ending. Use descriptive language to explain what happens to Yuki.

    _____

    _____

    _____

    _____

    _____

# Writing Assignment

To describe something, a writer uses interesting words to tell what he or she sees, hears, feels, tastes, and smells. The writer also compares things to other things, like a forest to a runny watercolor. Describe something that you and a relative or friend did together. Use this writing plan to help you write.

## Writing Plan

 **Directions** ➤ What experience would you like to describe? Write it in the circle. Then write words, similes, or metaphors that describe the experience on the lines.

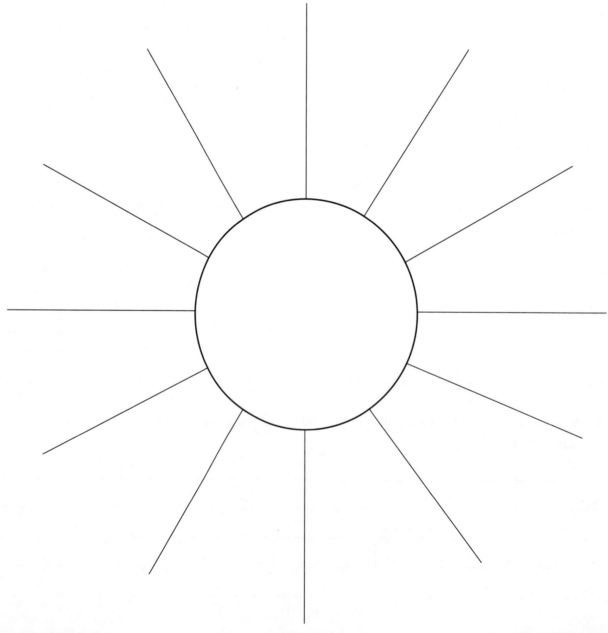

# First Draft

Tips for Writing a Descriptive Story:

- Use your *voice* when you write. That means you should use your special way of expressing yourself.

- Help readers see, smell, taste, feel, and hear what you are writing about.

- Use interesting words to help you describe.

- Use similes and metaphors to help your readers imagine the experience you are writing about.

## First Draft

**Directions** → Use your writing plan as a guide as you write your first draft of a *Descriptive Story*.

_____

_____

_____

_____

_____

_____

_____

_____

_____

_____

_____

_____

_____

*(Continue on your own paper.)*

# Revise the Draft

**Directions** ▷ Use the chart below to help you revise your draft. Check *Yes* or *No* to answer each question in the chart. If you answer *No*, make notes to remind yourself how you can revise, or change, your writing to improve it.

| Question | Yes ✔ | No ✔ | If the answer is no, what will you do to improve your writing? |
|---|---|---|---|
| Do you focus on something that happened to you and a relative or friend? | | | |
| Do you describe what you see, hear, smell, taste, and feel? | | | |
| Do you use action words to describe what happens? | | | |
| Do you use descriptive similes and metaphors? | | | |
| Do you describe events in the order they happen? | | | |
| Have you corrected mistakes in spelling, grammar, and punctuation? | | | |

**Directions** ▷ Use the notes in your chart and writing plan to revise your draft.

Name _____     Date _____

# Writing Report Card

**Directions** > Read your revised draft again or ask someone else to read it. Have the person who reads your paper complete the following Report Card. Revise your paper until you have no less than a Very Good Score for each item.

Title of paper: _____

Purpose of paper: _____ This paper is a descriptive story. It describes ____ something a friend or relative and I did together. ____

Person who scores the paper: _____

| Score | Writing Goals |
|---|---|
| | Does this story describe an experience that happened to the writer and a friend or relative? |
| | Does the writer describe what he or she sees, hears, tastes, smells, and feels? |
| | Does the writer use interesting action words? |
| | Does the story include descriptive similes and metaphors? |
| | Are the events that happen in the story in order? |
| | Are the story's grammar, spelling, and punctuation correct? |

☺ Excellent Score     ☆ Very Good Score     + Good Score

✔ Acceptable Score     — Needs Improvement

Writing Skills 8, SV 6508-0

Name _____     Date _____

# A Model Paper

## A How-to Paper

### *Make Your Own Sundial*

Have you ever wondered how people told time before the invention of the wind-up clock or the digital watch? In ancient times, people used something called a sundial, or shadow clock, for keeping time. The first sundial was probably just a simple pole or stick in the ground. People looked at the direction and length of the shadow cast by the stick to determine the time of day.

You may have observed that at sunrise your shadow is very long. In fact, it's longer than you are. And, you may have seen that at sunset your shadow is long, too. But it points the other way. In the middle of the day, the Sun is highest in the sky. Then your shadow is very short. It looks like a small dark spot around your feet.

Think of yourself as the pin of a sundial. As the pin, you cast a shadow. The pin on a sundial works the same way. The pin sits in the middle of a flat plate, which is marked with hours of the day. The directions *North* and *South* are marked on the plate.

The pin's shadow changes throughout the day. The length of the shadow depends on the height and angle of the Sun. As the Sun moves across the sky, the pin's shadow falls on each hour of the day, showing the time.

By 2000 B.C., people in Egypt and China were making sundials that could be carried from place to place. More advanced forms of the sundial were developed by the Greeks and Romans around 600 B.C. They created bowl-shaped dials with hour lines marked in the hollow of the bowl. The Romans even made sundials that could be worn as rings or on wristbands. But there was a problem. There were no shadows on cloudy days, making it hard to tell the time from season to season.

You can make your own sundial, with just a few simple materials. They include:
- a watch or clock
- glue
- a paper plate
- a long, sharpened pencil
- a ruler
- an empty thread spool
- a compass
- a marker

After you gather the necessary materials, you are ready to make a sundial. First, glue the spool to the middle of the paper plate. Then, stand the long, sharpened pencil in the hole of the spool, with the pencil's eraser on the bottom. This pencil is your pin. (Be careful when working with the sharpened pencil to avoid injuring your eyes or skin.) Next, use the marker to draw a mark anywhere on the edge of the plate. Label this mark with an *S* for *south*. This mark will be used to align your sundial with Earth's axis.

Find a window or a spot outdoors that is in full sunlight all day. Put the sundial in this sunny spot after sunrise. Then, use a compass to make sure the *S* label points south. This label keeps your sundial in the same relationship to the Earth and the Sun all day long. When your watch reaches the nearest hour, use the ruler to draw a straight line along the length of the shadow cast by the pin. Label the hour next to the line you drew. For example, when your watch reads 8 A.M., draw your line along the pin's shadow and label it *8 A.M.* Hint: To make it easier to draw on, you may want to place the paper plate on a hard surface, like a clipboard.

Repeat this step every hour, keeping the *S* label pointing south. Check the time, draw along the pin's shadow, and label the line with the hour. The last line you draw on your sundial is the last hour before the Sun sets.

When you have a line for each hour of sunlight, your sundial is finished. You can put it anywhere in the Sun, making sure the *S* label always points south. The pin's shadow will point to the hour of the day.

You can make your sundial more permanent by using a cement stepping stone instead of a paper plate. Use your imagination! Decorate the lines on the dial with bits of tile or small stones. Paint the spool and pencil with an enamel paint to make it weatherproof. Follow the example of early Romans and use Roman numerals to mark the hours. Place your finished sundial in a garden spot and always know what time it is. Unless, of course, it rains.

# Respond to the Model Paper

**Directions** ▷ Write your answers to the following questions or directions.

1. Why must the label *S* always point south?

   _____

   _____

   _____

2. Why must the sundial be placed in a sunny spot?

   _____

   _____

   _____

3. Why doesn't the sundial work in rainy weather?

   _____

   _____

   _____

4. Draw a picture of a sundial like the one the writer describes. Label the different hours on the dial. Decorate the sundial the way you would like it to look.

# Analyze the Model Paper

 **Directions** ⟩ Read "Make Your Own Sundial" again. As you read, think about why the writer wrote this paper. What did the writer do to help explain how a sundial works? Write your answers to the following questions or directions.

1.  Name at least two things that make this paper a good example of a how-to paper.

    _____

    _____

    _____

2.  Why does the writer list the materials you need to make a sundial before telling you how to do it?

    _____

    _____

    _____

3.  Why does the writer include the example and the hint in the seventh paragraph?

    _____

    _____

    _____

4.  Why does the writer use words like *first, then,* and *next*?

    _____

    _____

    _____

5.  The last paragraph serves more than one purpose. Name two things the writer achieves in the last paragraph.

    _____

    _____

    _____

Name _____  Date _____

# Writing Assignment

 **Directions** > Think about something you want to tell others how to do. Use this writing plan to help you write.

## Writing Plan

What will you tell others how to do?

List the materials someone will need.

Write the steps someone should follow in order. Number the steps.

Write some sequence words that help the reader know what to do.

# First Draft

Tips for Writing a How-to Paper:

● Choose one thing to teach someone.

● Focus on a plan.

    1. Think of all the materials someone will need.

    2. Think of all the steps someone will follow.

● Use sequence words in your directions.

## First Draft

**Directions** ⟩ Use your writing plan as a guide as you write your first draft of a *How-to Paper*.

_____

_____

_____

_____

_____

_____

_____

_____

_____

_____

_____

_____

_____

*(Continue on your own paper.)*

# Revise the Draft

**Directions** > Use the chart below to help you revise your draft. Check *Yes* or *No* to answer each question in the chart. If you answer *No*, make notes to remind yourself how you can revise, or change, your writing to improve it.

| Question | Yes ✔ | No ✔ | If the answer is no, what will you do to improve your writing? |
|---|---|---|---|
| Does your paper teach someone how to do something? | | | |
| Do you introduce the project or task in the first paragraph? | | | |
| Do you include safety warnings if they are necessary? | | | |
| Do you include all of the materials someone needs? | | | |
| Do you explain all of the steps someone must follow? | | | |
| Are the steps in order? | | | |
| Do you explain each step clearly so that it is easy to follow? | | | |
| Do you use sequence words to help guide your reader? | | | |
| Have you corrected mistakes in spelling, grammar, and punctuation? | | | |

**Directions** > Use the notes in your chart and writing plan to revise your draft.

# Writing Report Card

**Directions** ⟩ Read your revised draft again or ask someone else to read it. Have the person who reads your paper complete the following Report Card. Revise your paper until you have no less than a Very Good Score for each item.

Title of paper: _____

Purpose of paper: _____ This paper explains how to do something. _____

Person who scores the paper: _____

| Score | Writing Goals |
|---|---|
|  | Does the writer introduce the topic in the first paragraph? |
|  | Does the paper teach someone how to do something? |
|  | Does the paper include necessary safety warnings? |
|  | Does the paper include the materials someone needs? |
|  | Does the paper explain each step someone will follow? |
|  | Are the steps in order? |
|  | Is each step written clearly to make it easy to follow? |
|  | Are there sequence words to help the reader understand? |
|  | Are the paper's grammar, spelling, and punctuation correct? |

☺ Excellent Score     ☆ Very Good Score     + Good Score

✔ Acceptable Score     − Needs Improvement

# A Model Paper

## A Compare and Contrast Paper

## *Ride in Style*

Did you know that horses have been around since the time of dinosaurs? In fact, the horse is one of the oldest mammals in the world. Fifty million years ago, horses had four toes and were only eighteen inches high. That made them about as tall as a medium-size dog. Seven million years ago, horses had only one toe on each foot. They were also taller, about as big as modern-day horses. People tamed horses about nine thousand years ago and have been riding them ever since.

At first, learning to ride a horse was difficult. People were always falling off. Plus, they had nothing to protect their skin from rough horse hair. They didn't have shoes to protect their feet from the horse's sharp hooves, either. Over time, this changed. Nomads, or travelers, in ancient Asia invented stirrups, or footrests. These let riders stand up, turn, and duck down. Riders could also use them to make the horse jump and change direction.

Other inventions, such as saddles and horseshoes, let riders travel farther and do different kinds of work. The first horseshoes were actually shoes made from the hide of cows. The hide was tied onto the horse's hooves and left to dry. The Romans were the first to put metal shoes on horse's hooves.

Slowly, riding clothes changed, too. Pants made riding easier. Hard boots protected human feet from heavy horse hooves.

Today, there is a variety of clothing and tack, or equipment for riding horses. There are also two different styles of riding, called English and Western. Both styles have long histories. And both have their own clothing and tack, including saddles and reins.

English riding came to America from England in the 1600s. By the late 1700s, it was popular among wealthy Americans living in the eastern United States. These people thought the English way of riding was the proper way to ride. And riding became an important part of their social lives. People rode to visit friends, rode in hunting parties, and competed in horse shows.

The roots of Western riding can be traced back to the 1600s and 1700s. Cowboys called vaqueros worked on big Spanish ranches in the southwestern United States and northern Mexico. Western riding became more common in the middle and late 1800s. This was America's Wild West period. Cowboys and cowgirls worked hard and rode far in all kinds of weather. Many of them never left the saddle, doing all of their work from the back of a horse.

The ways riders sit and dress are different in English and Western riding. In English riding, the rider sits straight and tall in the saddle. He or she wears a black, flat-topped hat, a black long-tailed coat, white riding pants, and glossy black riding boots.

In Western riding, riders work with other animals, like cows or sheep. They must be able to move sideways, pull, chase, and do lots of messy work. As a result, their clothes are more practical. A rider wears a cowboy hat for shade. Blue jeans wear well through long hours of riding. Heavy, pointed boots protect toes and feet from the hooves of cattle or horses.

The English saddle was designed to be simple and light. The seat of the saddle is shaped to fit the horse and rider closely, so that they can move as one unit. Also, a light saddle means the horse has less weight to carry when it jumps.

The Western saddle has a horn in the front. This is a feature not found on English saddles. English riding requires lots of jumping. When a rider jumps, he or she must lean forward in the saddle. A saddle horn would get in the way. But cowboys and cowgirls use their horses and their saddles in other ways. The saddle horn gives a cowboy or cowgirl a strong object around which to tie a rope. Imagine a cowboy roping a steer. Once the rope slips over the steer's neck, the cowboy ties the end of the rope in his hand around the horn. This keeps the steer from slipping out of its noose or running away altogether.

The saddle horn is also handy when a cowboy or cowgirl needs to pull something, such as a fence post, using the horse's power. Horses used for Western riding are taught to walk backwards when they pull something so the rider can see what is happening. In Western riding, the horse and rider work as partners to get work done.

Western saddles are built with extra strong leather and stitching. This makes the saddle tough enough to stand up to hard use and bad weather. The seat of the Western saddle is designed for comfort, so the rider can work long hours in the saddle. Some cowboys and cowgirls slouch down and sleep on horseback if they have a long way to go, or if they have to stay with a cattle herd through the night.

Like the English saddle, English reins are simple, too. Reins are part of the bridle, or harness attached to a horse's head. They allow a rider to use his or her hands to "talk" to or control the horse. A rider holds one rein in each hand, controlling each move the horse makes. Control is especially important when a rider performs dressage. Dressage is a special kind of riding performed in horse shows. In dressage, a rider and horse move precisely. They also jump over low and high fences, hedges, and water.

In Western riding, a rider holds both reins in one hand. Keeping one hand free is important. The free hand can hold a whip to urge a horse forward or rope an animal, such as a stray calf.

People and horses share a long, rich history that continues to be written today. Riding styles, clothing, and tack will continue to change, but the amazing human and horse partnership remains the same.

# Respond to the Model Paper

**Directions** ▷ Write your answers to the following questions or directions.

1. How did the invention of stirrups help riders?

   _____

2. When did Western-style riding begin?

   _____

3. Summarize the story by making a chart. Use the chart below to list ways English and Western styles of riding are alike and different.

## A Compare and Contrast Chart
## for
## English and Western Styles of Riding

| How English and Western Styles of Riding Are Alike | How English and Western Styles of Riding Are Different |
|---|---|
| | |

# Analyze the Model Paper

 **Directions** ▷ Read "Ride in Style" again. As you read, think about how the writer achieved his or her purpose for writing. Write your answers to the following questions or directions.

1. Identify three important main ideas the writer uses to describe each style of riding.

   _____

   _____

   _____

   _____

2. Why do you think the writer uses the same main ideas to describe each style of riding?

   _____

   _____

   _____

   _____

3. Identify one important detail about each style of riding that supports the title of this paper.

   _____

   _____

   _____

4. How are the first and last paragraphs related? Why is this relationship important?

   _____

   _____

   _____

   _____

   _____

# Writing Assignment

 **Directions** Many people around the world have special relationships with different kinds of animals. In the United States, many people own dogs. Some are working dogs, such as dogs trained to assist blind people, police officers, or firefighters. Others serve as social companions to people in homes, schools, and hospitals. Learn more about how these dogs and their relationships with people are alike and how they are different. Use this writing plan to help plan your writing.

## Writing Plan

Choose two kinds of dogs you want to write about. Call them A and B.

A = _____          B = _____

Use what you know, books, or the Internet to learn more about the dogs you chose. Write the main ideas you will write about next to the heading *Main Idea*. For each main idea, list what is true only about A in the A circle. List what is true only about B in the B circle. List what is true about both A and B where the two circles overlap. If you have more than three main ideas, draw more diagrams on a separate sheet of paper.

**Main Idea:**

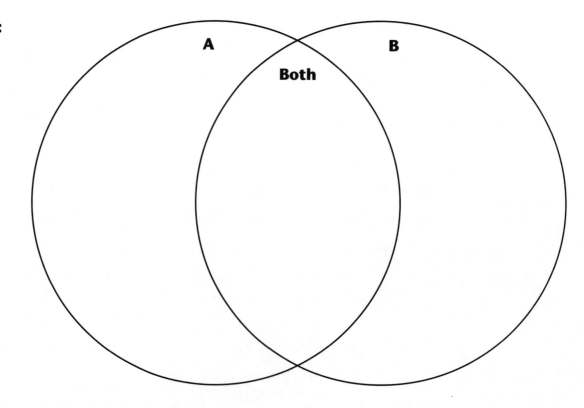

# Writing Assignment, page 2

**Main Idea:**

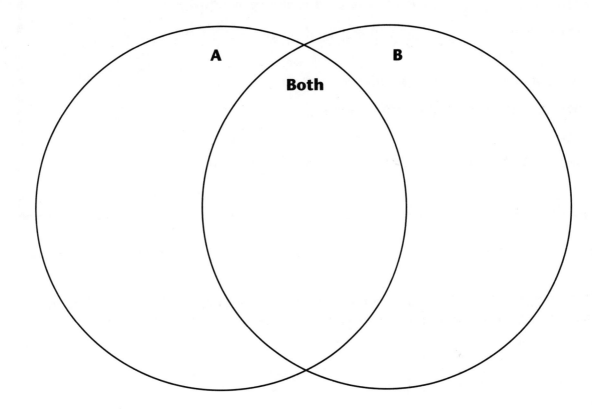

**Main Idea:**

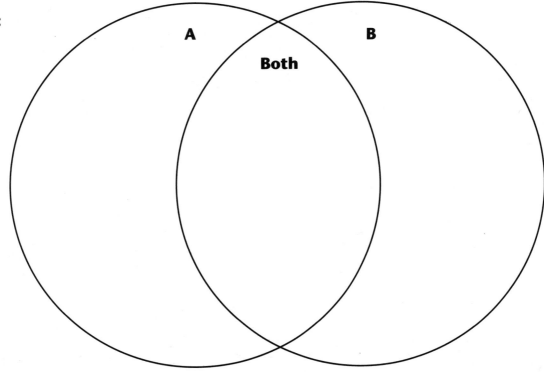

# First Draft

---

Tips for Writing a Compare and Contrast Paper:

- Find information about different kinds of dogs and their relationships with people.
- Organize the information you find into main ideas.
- Use details to explain each main idea.
- Explain how the dogs and relationships are alike.
- Explain how the dogs and relationships are different.
- Use your last paragraph to summarize your main ideas in a new way.

## First Draft

**Directions** ➤ Use your writing plan as a guide as you write your first draft of a *Compare and Contrast Paper*.

_____

_____

_____

_____

_____

_____

_____

_____

_____

_____

*(Continue on your own paper.)*

# Revise the Draft

**Directions** > Use the chart below to help you revise your draft. Check *Yes* or *No* to answer each question in the chart. If you answer *No*, make notes to remind yourself how you can revise, or change, your writing to improve it.

| Question | Yes ✔ | No ✔ | If the answer is no, what will you do to improve your writing? |
|---|---|---|---|
| Do you introduce the subjects you will write about in the first paragraph? | | | |
| Do you explain how the different kinds of dogs and relationships are alike? | | | |
| Do you explain how the different kinds of dogs and relationships are different? | | | |
| Do you have more than one main idea about the different kinds of dogs and relationships? | | | |
| Did you organize the main ideas into paragraphs? | | | |
| Do you use details to support each main idea? | | | |
| Do you summarize the main ideas of your paper in your conclusion? | | | |
| Have you corrected mistakes in spelling, grammar, and punctuation? | | | |

**Directions** > Use the notes in your chart and writing plan to revise your draft.

# Writing Report Card

**Directions** → Read your revised draft again or ask someone else to read it. Have the person who reads your paper complete the following Report Card. Revise your paper until you have no less than a Very Good Score for each item.

Title of paper: _____

Purpose of paper: _This paper shows how dogs and their relationships with people are alike and different._

Person who scores the paper: _____

| Score | Writing Goals |
|---|---|
| | Does the writer tell what the paper will be about in the first paragraph? |
| | Does the paper explain how the kinds of dogs and relationships are alike? |
| | Does the paper explain how the kinds of dogs and relationships are different? |
| | Does the writer use more than one main idea to describe the kinds of dogs and relationships? |
| | Does the writer include details to support each main idea? |
| | Does the writer organize the paragraphs in a way that makes sense? |
| | Does the last paragraph summarize what the paper is about? |
| | Are the paper's grammar, spelling, and punctuation correct? |

☺ Excellent Score      ★ Very Good Score      + Good Score

✔ Acceptable Score      − Needs Improvement

# A Model Paper

## A Short Report

## *A Home Away From Home*

The International Space Station (ISS) is the combined work of women and men from sixteen countries. They have come together to place a special community of scientists in orbit 250 miles above Earth. The participating countries are the United States, Russia, Canada, Japan, Brazil, and the European Space Agency (Belgium, Britain, Denmark, France, Germany, Italy, the Netherlands, Norway, Spain, Sweden, and Switzerland). These countries are spending billions of dollars, working for years, and facing the dangers of space to build the space station. Why? Because they believe the benefits of the space station will outweigh the huge costs.

The ISS is like a giant puzzle that is being put together high above Earth. The first piece of this puzzle is a Russian module, or section, called *Zarya. Zarya* was delivered into orbit November 20, 1998. Two weeks later, on December 4, 1998, the United States module *Unity* was launched into space. On December 7, 1998, *Zarya* and *Unity* were joined. More than 100 pieces must be built and shipped to Russia or the United States. Then, these pieces must be launched into space and joined before the station is complete. Building is expected to continue until April 2006.

Building a space station that is more than 600 feet long and weighs more than one million pounds is a big job. All together, there will be 46 launches. They include 37 U.S. space shuttle launches and nine Russian launches. When they arrive at the orbiting building site, astronaut teams will make at least 160 space walks to put the pieces together. They do this, of course, while the space station is moving at 17,500 miles per hour. That means that the station orbits Earth once every 90 minutes.

On their way to the ISS, astronauts wear special space suits. Inside the space station, astronauts wear regular clothing. But they must wear pressurized space suits during space walks. These suits are able to withstand flying debris. They also protect the astronauts from dramatic temperature changes. Temperatures outside the station can range from 120 degrees below Fahrenheit in the station's shadow to 250 degrees in the sun.

When the ISS is finished, people from around the world will live and work there for long periods of time. Scientists will study the effects of zero gravity on plants, animals, chemical processes, and humans.

Zero gravity causes human bones and muscles to become weaker. This weakness can be seen in astronauts who return from long stays in space. They are sometimes unable to walk without help. If humans are going to live in space, scientists need to know more about the effects of zero gravity on the human body. The ISS will let scientists study these effects and develop solutions for problems that come with spending a lot of time in space.

Zero gravity also causes changes in chemical processes. This means that new drugs and materials can be created and tested only in space. The cure for the common cold, for example, might be found in space. Scientists aboard the ISS may create new combinations of metals for building homes on Earth.

Living and working in space will certainly be different from life on Earth. But the ISS has been designed for comfort. It is divided into living areas that are roomy and bright. Temperatures are kept at a constant 70 degrees Fahrenheit. Comfort is important because astronauts will be busy. In a typical workday, they will spend 14 hours working and exercising, 1.5 hours preparing and eating meals, and 8.5 hours sleeping.

Because of zero gravity, exercise is even more important on the ISS than it is on Earth. To fight the loss of muscles and bones, astronauts on the station must exercise. They will use bikes, rowing machines, and other equipment for about two hours every day.

For meals, astronauts will have a galley, or special dining room. In early space missions, astronauts ate meats and vegetables that looked like baby food. Today, space food looks like food we enjoy on Earth. Plus, the ISS has water, microwave ovens, and refrigerators. This lets astronauts eat more familiar types of food, including fruit, vegetables, and even ice cream!

Each astronaut will have a private room, or berth. With no gravity, there is no need for a regular bed. A sleeping bag keeps each astronaut from floating away. That might sound like a strange way to sleep, but astronauts from past space missions say that they enjoy sleeping in space.

Zero gravity makes simple tasks like brushing teeth a lot harder. Water doesn't flow in a stream. It forms bubbles. Astronauts will use a closed shower and vacuum to catch the bath water. To go to the bathroom in space, astronauts will use a special air toilet that uses flowing air instead of water to get rid of waste.

The International Space Station will become a new moon above Earth, seen even during the day. A glance upward at the sky will remind us that humans have finally built a home away from home. The ISS will also be a reminder of the creative work that people from different countries can do when they work together.

Name _____   Date _____

# Respond to the Model Paper

**Directions** > Write your answers to the following questions or directions.

1.  What countries are involved in building the International Space Station?

    _____

    _____

    _____

2.  Why do astronauts wear a space suit during space walks?

    _____

    _____

3.  How would you describe a typical day for an astronaut aboard the space station?

    _____

    _____

    _____

4.  Write a paragraph to summarize the report. Use these questions to help you write your summary:

    • Who is involved in building the International Space Station?
    • What is required before building is complete?
    • What will life be like for astronauts living aboard the station?

    _____

    _____

    _____

    _____

    _____

    _____

    _____

    _____

# Analyze the Model Paper

**Directions** ▷ Read "A Home Away From Home" again. As you read, think about the main ideas the writer tells about. Write your answers to the following questions.

1. Why do you think the writer names all of the countries involved in building the first International Space Station in the first paragraph?

_____

_____

_____

2. What simile does the writer use in the second paragraph? Why do you think the writer decided to use this particular simile?

_____

_____

_____

3. Why does the writer include so many dates and measurements in the report?

_____

_____

_____

4. How is the first paragraph related to the last paragraph? Why is this relationship important?

_____

_____

_____

_____

_____

# Writing Assignment

In a short report, writers write about one topic. They find information about the topic. Then they use the information to choose the main ideas for their report. They also choose details to help explain each main idea.

 **Directions** ⟩ Write a short report about a science topic that interests you. Your idea might even come from the report "A Home Away From Home." Use this writing plan to help plan your writing.

## Writing Plan

The topic of this paper is:

_____

Main Idea of Paragraph 1: _____

Detail: _____

Detail: _____

Detail: _____

Main Idea of Paragraph 2: _____

Detail: _____

Detail: _____

Detail: _____

Main Idea of Paragraph 3: _____

Detail: _____

Detail: _____

Detail: _____

# First Draft

## Tips for Writing a Short Report:

- Find information about your topic.
- Take notes about main ideas important to your topic.
- Take notes about important details for each main idea.
- Organize the main ideas and details into paragraphs.
- Put paragraphs in a logical order.
- Use the last paragraph to summarize your report.

## First Draft

**Directions** ▷ Use your writing plan as a guide as you write your first draft of a *Short Report*.

_____

_____

_____

_____

_____

_____

_____

_____

_____

_____

*(Continue on your own paper.)*

Name _____    Date _____

# Revise the Draft

**Directions** ▷ Use the chart below to help you revise your draft. Check *Yes* or *No* to answer each question in the chart. If you answer *No*, make notes to remind yourself how you can revise, or change, your writing to improve it.

| Question | Yes ✔ | No ✔ | If the answer is no, what will you do to improve your writing? |
|---|---|---|---|
| Does your report focus on one topic? | | | |
| Do you introduce your topic in the first paragraph? | | | |
| Do you have more than one main idea to explain your topic? | | | |
| Do you organize your main ideas into paragraphs? | | | |
| Do you include details to explain each main idea? | | | |
| Do you use your last paragraph to summarize your report? | | | |
| Have you corrected mistakes in spelling, grammar, and punctuation? | | | |

**Directions** ▷ Use the notes in your chart and writing plan to revise your draft.

Name _____    Date _____

# Writing Report Card

**Directions** ▷ Read your revised draft again or ask someone else to read it. Have the person who reads your paper complete the following Report Card. Revise your paper until you have no less than a Very Good Score for each item.

Title of paper: _____

Purpose of paper: ___ **This paper is a short report.** _____

Person who scores the paper: _____

| Score | Writing Goals |
|---|---|
| | Does this short report focus on one topic? |
| | Does the writer introduce the topic of this paper in the first paragraph? |
| | Does the writer use more than one main idea to explain the topic? |
| | Are main ideas organized into paragraphs? |
| | Are there details to explain each main idea? |
| | Does the report "stick" to the topic? |
| | Does the last paragraph summarize the report? |
| | Are the report's grammar, spelling, and punctuation correct? |

☺ Excellent Score      ☆ Very Good Score      + Good Score

✔ Acceptable Score      − Needs Improvement

# A Model Paper

## A Persuasive Letter

Springfield High School
1015 Second Avenue
Springfield, Texas 75909

January 6, 2003

Dr. J. Reese
Superintendent, Springfield School District
1000 Main Street
Springfield, Texas 75909

Dear Dr. Reese:

   Many parents, teachers, and kids believe that homework has gotten out of hand.
Recently, our local newspaper printed an article by Janie McKee. She gave the results
of a homework study done at the University of Texas. Did you know that today's primary
school children do more homework than ever before? A first-grade student spends more
than six hours each week doing homework. That's 44 more minutes of homework than
students had in 1981. Even more surprising, older elementary students sit down to more
than ten hours of homework a week. That's about three hours more than students had
in 1981. Plus, today's kids spend many hours a week doing other school activities, such
as band, choir, sports, and drill team. All of these hours add up. Now you know why
family time has almost disappeared.
   I would like to suggest that our school district join the national movement called
"Take a Night Off From School." Joining this program would give families at least one
night to spend together. This would help free them from the stress of doing math
problems, history reports, and other school projects.
   Ms. McKee's article quoted Dr. Harris Miller, a professor at the University of Texas.
Dr. Miller said too much homework has "negative results." It upsets kids and makes them
feel bad about themselves when they don't have enough time to be part of important
family activities. Dr. Miller points out that the National Parent-Teacher Association
suggests a ten-minute homework rule. That rule says that kids should have ten minutes of
homework times their grade level. For example, a first grader should have ten minutes of
homework. As an eighth-grader, I should have no more than eighty minutes. That is one

hour and twenty minutes of homework each night! Dr. Miller also points out that some students have less homework than this. Some students, like me, for example, have much more. My classmates and I believe this is a serious problem. So do our parents and many of our teachers.

At this time, our district does not have rules regarding the amount of homework students should have each day. Without rules, teachers often assign only ten minutes of homework on Monday, but three hours on Thursday. This hurts not only students but parents as well. Family activities are hard to plan because the amount of homework on any night changes without warning. Homework limits would help solve this problem.

As a first step, I ask that you consider the "Take a Night Off From School" program. This national program encourages school districts to have one homework-free night each week. Recently, students, parents, and teachers in Sutton, New Jersey, had a successful homework-free night. There, school and community leaders worked together to pick a night for a "homework holiday." They chose a night with few or no scheduled community events. School and community leaders encouraged families to use the time to share dinner, visit a park, or play games together. The New Jersey "night off" was a big success. Now families have their community's support and encouragement to plan more family activities.

If you would like to know more about this successful national program, I would be happy to send more information. And, as a representative of the Student Council, let me assure you that our school and the P.T.A. would be happy to work with you. Plus, a representative of the "Take a Night Off From School" national organization has written to say she is willing to help our district. She will help plan and get community support for its first homework-free night. Working together, I know that we can begin to balance the needs of families with the need for a good education. I look forward to working with you.

Respectfully yours,

*Chantal Warden*

Chantal Warden
President
Springfield Student Council

# Respond to the Model Paper

**Directions** ▷ Write your answers to the following questions or directions.

1. Why is Chantal writing to the school superintendent?

_____

_____

2. List three reasons Chantal gives to explain why the school superintendent should consider the "Take a Night Off From School" event.

_____

_____

_____

3. According to Chantal, how many minutes of homework should an eighth-grade student expect each night?

_____

_____

4. Write a paragraph to summarize the main points Chantal makes in her letter. Use these questions to help you write your summary:

   • Why is Chantal writing?
   • What reasons for taking a night off from school does Chantal give the school superintendent?
   • How does Chantal support her recommendation to the superintendent?

_____

_____

_____

_____

_____

_____

_____

_____

# Analyze the Model Paper

 **Directions** ⟩ Read the persuasive letter from Chantal again. As you read, think about why she wrote this letter. Write your answers to the following questions or directions.

1.  Chantal doesn't introduce her reason for writing until the second paragraph. Why do you think she decided to use her first paragraph for another purpose?

    _____

    _____

    _____

2.  Why does Chantal quote Professor Miller in her letter to the superintendent?

    _____

    _____

    _____

3.  What does Chantal say in her last paragraph to convince the superintendent to pay close attention to her request?

    _____

    _____

    _____

    _____

4.  In her closing, Chantal uses the words "Respectfully yours." Why do you think Chantal used this phrase?

    _____

    _____

    _____

    _____

# Writing Assignment

**Directions** ➤ In a persuasive letter, a writer tries to convince someone or a group of people to do something. The writer tries to make the reader feel a certain emotion about the topic he or she writes about. Write a persuasive letter to a friend to convince him or her to join you and your family for a summer vacation. Use this writing plan to help you write.

## Writing Plan

**1.** Write your address.

**2.** Write the date.

**3.** Write your friend's name and address.

**4.** Write a polite greeting, or salutation.

**5.** What will you say in the first paragraph to let your friend know why you are writing?

**6.** Complete the chart.

| Main Points You Will Present | Supporting Details You Will Use |
|---|---|
|  |  |

**7.** Use your last paragraph to write a conclusion. Summarize the important points you made.

**8.** Choose a friendly closing.

# First Draft

## Tips for Writing a Persuasive Letter:

- Use a strong beginning to grab your reader's attention.
- Make your purpose for writing clear to the reader.
- Give reasons that will appeal to your reader's emotions.
- Organize your reasons into their order of importance.
- Organize your reasons from least important to most important.
- Use a strong ending that leaves your reader convinced you are right.

## First Draft

**Directions** ⟩ Use your writing plan as a guide for writing your first draft of a *Persuasive Letter.*

_____

_____

_____

_____

_____

_____

_____

_____

_____

_____

*(Continue on your own paper.)*

Name _____     Date _____

# Revise the Draft

**Directions** > Use the chart below to help you revise your draft. Check *Yes* or *No* to answer each question in the chart. If you answer *No*, make notes to remind yourself how you can revise, or change, your writing to improve it.

| Question | Yes ✔ | No ✔ | If the answer is no, what will you do to improve your writing? |
|---|---|---|---|
| Is the purpose of this letter clear? | | | |
| Does the first paragraph grab your reader's attention? | | | |
| Do you give specific reasons to convince your reader? | | | |
| Are the reasons you use in order from the least to the most important? | | | |
| Do you appeal to your reader's emotions? | | | |
| Do you use the last paragraph to restate your opinion in a convincing way? | | | |
| Have you corrected mistakes in spelling, grammar, and punctuation? | | | |

**Directions** > Use the notes in your chart and writing plan to revise your draft.

# Writing Report Card

**Directions** Read your revised draft again or ask someone else to read it. Have the person who reads your paper complete the following Report Card. Revise your paper until you have no less than a Very Good Score for each item.

Title of paper: _____

Purpose of paper: ___ This is a persuasive letter. _____

Person who scores the paper: _____

| Score | Writing Goals |
|-------|---------------|
|  | Is the writer's purpose for writing clear? |
|  | Does the writer grab the reader's attention in the first paragraph? |
|  | Does the writer give specific reasons to convince the reader? |
|  | Are reasons presented in order from the least to the most important? |
|  | Does the writer appeal to the reader's emotions? |
|  | Does the last paragraph leave the reader convinced the writer is right? |
|  | Are the letter's grammar, spelling, and punctuation correct? |

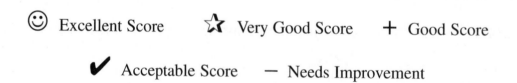

☺ Excellent Score     ☆ Very Good Score     + Good Score

✔ Acceptable Score     − Needs Improvement

# A Model Paper

## A Persuasive Movie Review

### *Professor Yomi's Class*

Fans of Anime, or Japanese animation, buckle your seat belts! Get ready to blast off! The latest science fiction film from the East is here, and Earth is in trouble *again!* In this movie, cartoon characters battle aliens who want to take over Earth. If you love Anime, the film *Professor Yomi's Class* is a treat. It comes out on videotape and on DVD later this summer.

It is 2123 and scientists are puzzled because they have not found signs of intelligent life in the universe. The film's hero, Professor Yomi, picks up strange noises coming from outer space. The World Space Agency (WSA) believes the noises are unimportant, but Professor Yomi knows better.

Professor Yomi and his students, Pikka, Lee, Rachel, and clever 11-year-old Katya, have been studying the stars and planets in their science class. With the help of a supercomputer called Cherub, the group finds that aliens have been "phoning home" for ages. But we just haven't been listening. The alien side to this story is that the ETs (extraterrestrials) haven't discovered our "simple" means of communication either. That is, until now. When the Professor and his class listen in on cosmic conversations, they discover that Earth is in serious danger! Meanwhile, it turns out that a group of not-so-nice aliens called the MALA know that Professor Yomi and his class have been listening.

Our group of heroes decides there's only one way to save Earth from doom. They must contact the MALA. So they dress up and talk like a group of Teef. The Teef are another group of aliens that the Professor has just discovered. Disguised as Teef, the class erases the MALA's knowledge of Earth. How WSA, the Professor, and the students work this out gets a little confusing at times. But the plot is strong, so you won't lose interest.

The real hero of the movie is Cherub, the computer. Cherub always comes through in the nick of time and acts as teacher and friend to the kids. The kids in Professor Yomi's class each have different skills and talents. That makes them fun to get to know and to follow to the end of the story. Another strength of the movie is that the Professor and the kids rely more on their brains than on force to solve their problems. Most fight scenes pit machines against machines, not people against aliens. This is a welcome change from most of the alien movies on the screen today.

For those of you who are new to Anime, there are two types of Japanese cartoon art. They are Manga and Anime. Manga is more like the art you find in a comic strip. It uses simple lines and repeats certain styles that make it different from other kinds of art.

Some people think that Anime is more artistic than Manga. It is most often compared to ancient Japanese art, art that dates back thousands of years. It borrows the traditional love of water scenes and mountains. *Professor Yomi's Class* is a good example. This Anime film creates space that isn't too dark to see what is going on. The artwork is exciting and colorful, and the background scenery is beautiful.

This is the first of four films planned for the *Professor Yomi's Class* series. So the film's makers take time to create the background and characters for the films that will follow. It is clear, however, that four films may not be enough to tell the whole story. Space seems full of strange, nasty aliens. The plucky characters in Professor Yomi's class could stay busy for many more movies to come.

The DVD comes in English, Japanese, Spanish, and French language versions. It's a kick to compare the actor's voices in the different languages. DVD is definitely the way to go, and the index lets you explore lots of interesting stuff. There is not only information about the real search for aliens, but also the World Space Agency, the MALA and Teef, and 3-D models of alien spaceships. The index also offers details on our solar system and the latest photos taken by the Hubble telescope. Best of all, there is a section on the history of Japanese animation that shows some of the well-known Anime characters and their authors.

I recommend *Professor Yomi's Class* to Anime lovers. I also recommend it to movie lovers interested in giving Japanese animation and science fiction another chance. Professor Yomi made me laugh out loud! I look forward to seeing how the computer Cherub and the likeable Katya keep us from future destruction. Pass the popcorn, please!

# Respond to the Model Paper

**Directions** > Write your answers to the following questions or directions.

1.  Name the important characters in this movie.

    _____

    _____

2.  Summarize the movie's plot.

    _____

    _____

    _____

    _____

3.  Describe the two kinds of Japanese cartoon art.

    _____

    _____

    _____

4.  Write a paragraph to summarize this movie review. Use these questions to help you write your summary:

    • What is the purpose of this review?
    • What reasons does the writer give to convince readers to see this movie?

    _____

    _____

    _____

    _____

    _____

    _____

    _____

    _____

# Analyze the Model Paper

 **Directions** ⟩ Read the review of *Professor Yomi's Class* again. As you read, think about how the writer convinces readers to see this movie. Write your answers to the following questions or directions.

1.  What does the writer do in the first paragraph to grab readers' attention?

    _____

    _____

    _____

    _____

2.  Why do you think the writer takes time to summarize the movie's plot?

    _____

    _____

    _____

    _____

3.  Read the ninth paragraph again. Why do you think the writer included this information?

    _____

    _____

    _____

    _____

4.  What do the first and last paragraphs have in common? Why is this relationship important?

    _____

    _____

    _____

    _____

# Writing Assignment

 **Directions** ➤ In a persuasive movie review, writers try to convince readers to watch a movie. What's your favorite movie? Write a persuasive movie review to convince your friends to see this movie.

## Writing Plan

What is the name of the movie you will review?

_____

Write reasons your friends should see this movie. Write details to support each reason.

**Reason #1**

_____

_____

**Reason #2**

_____

_____

**Details to support Reason #1**

_____

_____

_____

**Details to support Reason #2**

_____

_____

_____

**Reason #3**

_____

_____

**Reason #4**

_____

_____

**Details to support Reason #3**

_____

_____

_____

**Details to support Reason #4**

_____

_____

_____

# First Draft

Tips for Writing a Persuasive Movie Review:

● Make sure you have a strong opinion.

● Give good reasons to support your opinion.

● Give important details that support each reason.

● Grab your reader's attention in the first paragraph.

● Restate your opinion in the last paragraph.

## First Draft

**Directions** ⟩ Use your writing plan as a guide for writing your first draft of a *Persuasive Movie Review*.

_____

_____

_____

_____

_____

_____

_____

_____

_____

_____

_____

_____

_____

*(Continue on your own paper.)*

# Revise the Draft

**Directions** ➤ Use the chart below to help you revise your draft. Check *Yes* or *No* to answer each question in the chart. If you answer *No*, make notes to remind yourself how you can revise, or change, your writing to improve it.

| Question | Yes ✔ | No ✔ | If the answer is no, what will you do to improve your writing? |
|---|---|---|---|
| Do you use your first paragraph to grab the reader's attention? | | | |
| Do you make it clear that you have a strong opinion? | | | |
| Do you give good reasons to support your opinion? | | | |
| Do you include details that help support each reason? | | | |
| Do you restate your opinion in the last paragraph? | | | |
| Does this review make your reader want to see this movie? | | | |
| Have you corrected mistakes in spelling, grammar, and punctuation? | | | |

**Directions** ➤ Use the notes in your chart and writing plan to revise your draft.

Name _____ Date _____

# Writing Report Card

**Directions** Read your revised draft again or ask someone else to read it. Have the person who reads your paper complete the following Report Card. Revise your paper until you have no less than a Very Good Score for each item.

Title of paper: _____

Purpose of paper: ___ This paper is a persuasive movie review. _____

Person who scores the paper: _____

| Score | Writing Goals |
|-------|---------------|
| | Does the first paragraph grab the reader's attention? |
| | Is the writer's opinion clearly stated? |
| | Does the writer give good reasons for his or her opinion? |
| | Are there details to support each reason? |
| | Does the writer restate his or her opinion in the last paragraph? |
| | Does this review make you want to see this movie? |
| | Are the review's grammar, spelling, and punctuation correct? |

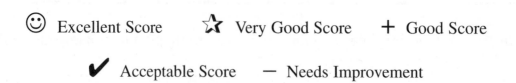

☺ Excellent Score ☆ Very Good Score + Good Score

✔ Acceptable Score − Needs Improvement

# A Model Paper

## A Persuasive Essay

### *Reduce, Reuse, Recycle*

All across the United States, local governments are faced with the same growing problem—garbage. What is garbage, or trash? It's waste from our homes, businesses, schools, and hospitals. It's the stuff we don't need anymore. It's things we call useless. Americans produce nearly 210 million tons of solid waste each year! Then they demand that their cities find places to store it.

Finding cheap landfills, or places to put our mounting trash, is only part of the problem. People who work in landfills want more money. Plus, new laws add to the cost of storing garbage. These laws are meant to keep groundwater safe and reduce methane, the dangerous gas that comes from landfills. But they also mean we pay more to have our trash picked up and hidden.

People argue about how to solve the garbage problem. Some think we should build more and bigger landfills. Others think we should dump trash in the ocean. Still others say we should build expensive power plants that burn trash for energy. However, many experts think that the best long-term answer is something called the triangle of the three Rs. The three Rs stand for *Reduce, Reuse, Recycle.* Together, the experts say, these three Rs are the solution to our garbage problem.

Let's look at the first two Rs in the triangle—Reduce and Reuse. We often overlook ways to reduce and reuse solid waste. But if we are going to manage our trash, reducing and reusing are more important than recycling. We reduce our trash when we buy and use fewer things. That's because in time, the things themselves become trash. So does the material that was used to wrap them.

Consider ways you can reduce your trash. One way is to buy concentrated items. For example, when you buy orange juice, buy the concentrated kind. Concentrated juice is usually packaged in a small, paper container. You add water at home. The people who sell unconcentrated juice add water before they package the juice. You pay extra for the water and the larger, plastic container used to hold it.

Buying food or materials in bulk also cuts down on trash. This means that when you buy one huge bag of rice, for example, you make less trash than when you buy lots of smaller bags.

Another way to reduce your trash is in your yard. There you can build a compost pile. Compost is a mix of food waste from your kitchen and cut grass from your lawn. Stirring the compost helps it decay, or break down. Then you can add it to your yard or garden plants to help feed them and keep them moist. It also protects them from cold temperatures. Keeping a compost pile means usable plant waste stays at home instead of taking up space at a landfill.

Reusing is just as important as reducing the number of products we buy. Replace paper cups with china cups that can be used again and again. Carry cloth grocery bags to the grocery store. If you buy soda at the movies, pay attention to the specials. Some theaters sell plastic cups that you can use over and over again. And refills are cheaper.

Now let's look at the last R in the triangle—Recycling. Think for a moment about what you throw away in just one month. Chances are, if all of the trash you created were piled next to you, you would be standing next to a small mountain.

In 1988, the city of Phoenix paid for a garbage study. Leaders in the city wanted to know what people throw away. They hired Dr. Bill Rathje, of the University of Arizona Anthropology Department, to lead the study. Dr. Rathje and his team sorted and classified garbage from 500 homes. They learned that most of the garbage people threw away could be recycled. If we say that the trash in this study is like the trash we all throw away, almost 90 percent of the solid waste we create could be recycled. That means it never needs to reach the landfill!

Try as we might, we can throw out the garbage. We can carry it to the curb. And even take it to the dump. But we can never really make our own mountains of garbage disappear. When we throw garbage away, it just goes somewhere else, and at a cost. Until we use the three Rs, we are stuck with our trash.

Many cities are so short of landfill space that they give recycling bins to homes and businesses to shrink the amount of solid garbage waste they pick up. When you do something as simple as recycle a soda can, you help reduce the amount of aluminum that is taken from the ground. You also help reduce energy use and the water and air pollution that come from processing the aluminum.

In many older landfills, toxic, or poisonous, substances leak into the groundwater that we drink or use on our crops. Cleaning up these leaks can be costly. Prevention makes more sense, and that's where recycling comes in. When you recycle motor oil, for example, you help keep toxic substances like lead out of your local landfill. That means you help keep them out of your air and water, too.

Of all the environmental problems we face, garbage is one problem you can really do something about. The choices you make every day affect the amount of garbage you throw away and the environmental problems you help create. When you follow the three Rs—Reduce, Reuse, Recycle—you lessen waste and the problems that go with it. You save natural resources, decrease the need for energy, and reduce air, water, and land pollution. You also save money.

Garbage isn't just your problem, but you are an important part of the solution. Following the three Rs saves money, benefits the environment, and protects your health. So start using the three Rs to manage your own mountain of garbage. Conquer your mountain with a cry of "Reduce, Reuse, Recycle" that can be heard around the world.

# Respond to the Model Paper

**Directions** ➤ Write your answers to the following questions or directions.

1. How much solid waste do Americans produce in one year?

   _____

   _____

2. According to the writer, what do the words *landfill, compost,* and *decay* mean?

   _____

   _____

   _____

3. What is the "three-R" solution to garbage?

   _____

   _____

   _____

4. Write a paragraph to summarize this essay. Use these questions to help you write your summary:

   • What is the writer's position regarding garbage?
   • What details does the writer include to support his or her position?
   • How does the writer appeal to readers' emotions?

   _____

   _____

   _____

   _____

   _____

   _____

   _____

   _____

   _____

# Analyze the Writer's Model

 **Directions** ➤ Read "Reduce, Reuse, Recycle" again. As you read, think about the main ideas the writer discusses. Write your answers to the following questions or directions.

1. What is the tone of the writer's first paragraph?

   _____

   _____

   _____

2. Why does the writer give readers specific examples of opportunities to reduce, reuse, and recycle their garbage?

   _____

   _____

   _____

   _____

3. Read the first sentence in the fourteenth paragraph again. Why is this sentence important?

   _____

   _____

   _____

4. How are the first and last paragraphs related? Why is this relationship important?

   _____

   _____

   _____

   _____

   _____

Name _____    Date _____

# Writing Assignment

Before a writer begins to write a persuasive essay, he or she forms an opinion. This opinion becomes the writer's purpose for writing. Then the writer gives specific reasons why the reader should have the same opinion.

 **Directions** ⟩ Write a persuasive essay about a topic that is important to you. State your opinion clearly. Also offer important reasons for this opinion. Use this writing plan to help you write.

## Writing Plan

**What will the topic of your essay be?**              **What is your opinion on this topic?**

_____  ◀·▶  _____

**Reason 1**                                              **Why? Support your reason.**

```
_____          ◀·▶          _____
_____                               _____
_____                               _____
```

**Reason 2**                                              **Why? Support your reason.**

```
_____          ◀·▶          _____
_____                               _____
_____                               _____
```

**Reason 3**                                              **Why? Support your reason.**

```
_____          ◀·▶          _____
_____                               _____
_____                               _____
```

# First Draft

## Tips for Writing a Persuasive Essay:

- ● Grab your reader's attention in the first paragraph.
- ● State your opinion clearly.
- ● Support your opinion with clear examples.
- ● Present your examples from least important to most important.
- ● Use the last paragraph to summarize your report.
- ● Use your last paragraph to leave the reader convinced you are right.

## First Draft

**Directions** ⟩ Use your writing plan as a guide for writing your first draft of a *Persuasive Essay*.

_____

_____

_____

_____

_____

_____

_____

_____

_____

_____

_____

_____

_____

*(Continue on your own paper.)*

# Revise the Draft

**Directions** ⟩ Use the chart below to help you revise your draft. Check *Yes* or *No* to answer each question in the chart. If you answer *No*, make notes to remind yourself how you can revise, or change, your writing to improve it.

| Question | Yes ✔ | No ✔ | If the answer is no, what will you do to improve your writing? |
|---|---|---|---|
| Do you use your first paragraph to grab the reader's attention? | | | |
| Do you have a clear opinion? | | | |
| Do you include strong reasons that support your opinion? | | | |
| Do you organize your reasons from least to most important? | | | |
| Do you restate your opinion in the last paragraph? | | | |
| Do you use your last paragraph to leave your reader convinced that you are right? | | | |
| Have you corrected mistakes in spelling, grammar, and punctuation? | | | |

**Directions** ⟩ Use the notes in your chart and writing plan to revise your draft.

Name _____     Date _____

# Writing Report Card

**Directions** ➤ Read your revised draft again or ask someone else to read it. Have the person who reads your paper complete the following Report Card. Revise your paper until you have no less than a Very Good Score for each item.

Title of paper: _____

Purpose of paper: _____ This paper is a persuasive essay. _____

Person who scores the paper: _____

| Score | Writing Goals |
|---|---|
|  | Does the writer grab your attention right away? |
|  | Is the writer's opinion absolutely clear? |
|  | Does the writer include reasons that support his or her opinion? |
|  | Are the reasons organized from least to most important? |
|  | Does the last paragraph restate the writer's opinion in a new way? |
|  | Is the essay convincing? |
|  | Are the essay's grammar, spelling, and punctuation correct? |

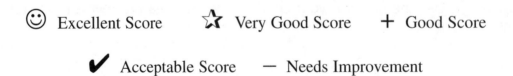

☺ Excellent Score     ☆ Very Good Score     + Good Score

✔ Acceptable Score     — Needs Improvement

# Writing Skills: Grade 8, Answer Key

Answers to some questions may vary, but examples are provided here to give you an idea of how students may respond. Encourage students to share, discuss, and evaluate their answers, particularly their summaries. Also, encourage students to answer all questions in complete sentences.

**page 22**

1. Jane describes herself as the new kid in school. She talks about how she is slow to make friends. She also suggests that she doesn't like to be the center of attention. She thinks of herself as independent since she dresses to suit her own likes and dislikes. Jane says she is not concerned with fitting in. She describes herself as slow to think of responses to teasing. Jane describes Madison as someone who is popular in school and as someone who looks like she just stepped out of a fashion magazine. She describes Madison as her "living nightmare" because Madison teases her so much and seems to be everywhere she is.

2. Jane misunderstands Madison's teasing and the reason for her squinting. Madison thinks Jane doesn't like the way she looks and dresses since Jane keeps her distance and dresses so differently. Madison doesn't understand that her family's style of teasing makes Jane feel picked on and that the teasing is the reason she stays away.

3. Help students summarize the significant events of the story, paraphrasing as needed. Summaries should be organized in a thoughtful way, with the main ideas and important details clearly presented.

**page 23**

1. Jane uses words like *I, me,* and *my* to show that she is writing about her personal experiences.

2. Jane is the new kid at Jordan Middle School, and she is having trouble fitting in. She is having particular trouble with one student, Madison James.

3. The writer uses some unusual metaphors to add humor and interest to the story. The writer also uses simile, such as in paragraph two: "I was as red as a late summer tomato."

4. The writer includes the novel as an interesting way for the two main characters to understand and confront their problems with each other.

**page 30**

1. The writer took a trip to Texas and learned how to appreciate another place and its culture.

2. The setting is West Texas. The land is less populated and more desert-like than the writer is used to.

3. In the ninth paragraph, the writer begins to notice the beauty and quiet of the landscape after the rain.

4. Check to see that students summarize the significant events of the story. Summaries should be organized in a thoughtful way, with the main ideas and important details clearly presented.

**page 31**

1. The story begins with a bus trip. The writer lets the reader know how he is feeling right away. The mood is gloomy. In the second paragraph, the writer shifts the mood and action by giving background information on how he came to be in Texas.

2. The writer says that he had never been outside New York before, and that "Texas seemed a million miles away." This implies that he will have to adjust to a very different place. Also, he doesn't answer yes or no to the invitation, and his parents think the experience will be good for him. This implies that he might have some problems with new experiences.

3. The writer uses the fresh-washed feeling after the storm to communicate that the mood is different.

4. The writer really lets the reader into his mind and feelings. His mood is different, he's reflective, and he says, "Maybe Texas wasn't so bad after all."

**page 38**

1. Yuki was hiking in a huge forest with trails and a swimming hole. The forest had tall pine trees and scrubby underbrush. There were rock outcroppings scattered through the woods.

2. Yuki was tired and grumpy and had an argument with her friend, Jada.

3. Yuki stayed behind at the rest spot and took a nap instead of hiking with the group.

4. Guide students in summarizing the significant events of the story. Summaries should be organized in a thoughtful way, with the main ideas and important details clearly presented.

# Writing Skills: Grade 8, Answer Key, continued

**page 39**

1. Drawings will vary, but look for an understanding of Yuki's predicament.

2. These descriptions help the reader feel the thirst and understand how Yuki's sunburned skin feels.

3. The writer describes the landscape as a watercolor seen through Yuki's tears. Another metaphor might be, "The forest began to slip sideways in an earthquake of tears."

4. Answers will vary, but look for an understanding of the plot and the descriptive mood of the story.

**page 46**

1. This aligns the sundial with the Earth's axis and gives it a consistent reference point.

2. The Sun is necessary to cast a shadow on the time markers.

3. The Sun is not shining on rainy days.

4. Drawings will vary, but look for indications of understanding and creativity.

**page 47**

1. The writer states the purpose of the paper clearly, lists the materials, gives clear, step-by-step instructions, and gives helpful hints and details.

2. The writer lists the materials so they can be collected before starting the project. That saves time and makes the project easier to do.

3. The example shows you more clearly how to label the dial. Hints give special guidance to the reader. In this case, it is a hint meant to help the reader label the sundial more easily.

4. Sequence words such as *first, next,* and *then* help the reader understand the order of the steps.

5. The last paragraph adds interest to the how-to paper by sparking the reader's imagination. It also gives some helpful hints on how to add some creative touches to the sundial. The paragraph ends with a little humor to keep the reader reading until the very last word.

**page 54**

1. Stirrups helped riders stand up, turn, and duck down while riding. The stirrups also helped riders to make their horses jump and change direction.

2. In the 1600s and 1700s, Western-style riding began in northern Mexico and in the southwestern United States. There, cowboys called vaqueros worked on big Spanish ranches. But Western-style riding became more established in the 1800s during America's Wild West period.

3. Guide students in organizing the information in a clear manner, using words and phrases that show comparisons and contrasts.

How English and Western Styles of Riding Are Alike: Both styles of riding have a long, interesting history.; Both styles have benefited from inventions designed in other countries.; Both styles have their own special tack, or equipment, that evolved over time.; Both styles have their own special clothing.; Both styles have saddles and reins with unique features.; Both require a special partnership between human and animal.

How English and Western Styles of Riding Are Different: English riding came to America from England.; Western riding originated in northern Mexico and in the southwestern United States.; English riding has a traditional, social purpose.; Western riding began as a working style that allowed riders to interact easily with other animals, such as cows and sheep.; In English riding, the rider sits up straight and tall.; In Western riding, the rider may slouch down for comfort during work.; English riders wear traditional clothes, such as a black hat, a long-tailed coat, white riding pants, and glossy black boots.; Western riders wear casual work clothes, such as jeans, a cowboy hat, and heavy pointed boots to protect their toes.; The English saddle has no horn and is simple and light and is designed for easy jumping.; The Western saddle is strong and has a saddle horn which is used to rope and pull. The Western saddle is built for comfort.; In English riding, the reins are designed to let the rider communicate with the horse, and both hands hold the reins.; In Western riding, the rider holds the reins in one hand to keep the other free for work.; Dressage is a kind of riding performed by English-style riders.

# Writing Skills: Grade 8, Answer Key, continued

**page 55**

1. The writer describes the special tack, or equipment, that is used, the unique clothing common to each style, and the unique purpose of each style of riding.

2. By using the same main ideas, the writer is able to give details about each riding style that can be compared or contrasted to the main points listed.

3. In English riding, the saddle is very light, and there is no saddle horn. This allows the rider to move with the horse while jumping. In Western-style riding, riders dress in their own casual style with broad hats for shade and blue jeans for protection.

4. The writer links the history of the horse with human history in both the first and the last paragraphs. This provides a strong framework for the paper by showing that both styles of riding depend on that special human and horse relationship.

**page 63**

1. The participating countries are the United States, Russia, Canada, Japan, Brazil, and the European Space Agency (Belgium, Britain, Denmark, France, Germany, Italy, the Netherlands, Norway, Spain, Sweden, and Switzerland).

2. These special pressurized space suits are designed to withstand flying debris and to protect the astronauts from temperature changes.

3. In a typical workday, astronauts will spend 14 hours working and exercising, 1.5 hours preparing and eating meals, and 8.5 hours sleeping.

4. Guide students in summarizing the report. Summaries should be organized in a thoughtful way, with the main ideas and important details clearly presented.

**page 64**

1. The writer wants to show that the ISS is a worldwide project that involves the creativity and commitment of many countries. The writer also shows the time and money commitments that all these countries are willing to make.

2. The writer compares the space station to a giant puzzle being assembled in Earth's orbit. This simile accurately expresses how the ISS is being assembled piece by piece.

3. The writer shows that this is a scientific project, concerned with scientific discoveries.

4. In the first paragraph, the writer outlines the sacrifices that the sixteen countries are making. In the last paragraph, the writer talks about what can be accomplished when so many people from so many different countries get together. The writer is emphasizing that the space station is a scientific world effort and is not the property of any one nation.

**page 71**

1. Chantal wants to persuade the superintendent to join the "Take a Night Off From School" movement. She would also like the school system to start a homework policy.

2. Chantal lists evidence that students are burdened with too much homework and too many school activities. She also mentions that families are losing valuable time together and that students are experiencing "negative results" because of the amount of homework.

3. As an eighth-grader, she should have no more than eighty minutes of homework, or ten minutes of homework times the grade level.

4. Guide students in summarizing the reasons Chantal gives to the superintendent. Summaries should be organized in a thoughtful way, with the main ideas and important details clearly presented.

# Writing Skills: Grade 8, Answer Key, continued

**page 72**

1. She uses a recent newspaper article to set up her reason for asking Dr. Reese to consider the "night off" from schoolwork and activities. The article lends support to her later argument.

2. Professor Miller holds a respected position. As an older person and an educator, his view that too much homework can have "negative results" adds more support to the case Chantal is making.

3. She lists the support she has already received for the idea of taking a night off. She mentions that the student council, the PTA, and the national "Take a Night Off From School" organization are ready and willing to lend support to the idea.

4. Chantal is showing respect for Dr. Reese's position and age and is more likely to win his support by recognizing his authority in this way.

**page 79**

1. The important characters are Professor Yomi and his students, Pikka, Lee, Rachel, and Katya, and the computer, Cherub.

2. It is the year 2123, and Professor Yomi and his class of students discover alien messages coming from outer space. The World Space Agency (WSA) thinks the messages are just space noise. In reality, they are alien coded messages. Some not-so-nice aliens, the MALA, catch the professor and his students listening to their transmissions. In order to save Earth from MALA's notice, the Professor, his students Pikka, Lee, Rachel, and Katya, and the computer, Cherub, disguise themselves as the Teef. The Teef are a harmless, recently discovered group of aliens who make their living by trading. The mission of Yomi's group is to erase MALA's knowledge of Earth.

3. Manga is more like comic-strip art, and it uses simple lines. Anime is more artistic and has elements of traditional Japanese scenes, such as mountains and water.

4. Check to see that students identify the purpose of the review and summarize its significant points. Summaries should be organized in a thoughtful way, with the main reasons for seeing the movie and the important details clearly presented.

**page 80**

1. The reviewer uses colorful language like "buckle your seat belts" and "get ready to blast off."

2. The reviewer wants to inform the reader and catch the reader's attention. A simple sketch of the movie plot is common in movie reviews.

3. The reviewer includes this information in order to educate his readers about what is special in the DVD version. He thinks it is the version that viewers would want to have.

4. The first and last paragraphs repeat the reviewer's opinion that this is a film that fans of Japanese animation and science fiction will love. In the last paragraph, he adds that people who have not liked animated science fiction before will like *Professor Yomi's Class*. He uses the same catchy, colorful language in both paragraphs. This gives a sense of unity and fun to the review.

**page 87**

1. Americans produce 210 million tons of solid waste each year.

2. A landfill is a place to put trash. Compost is a mix of food waste from the kitchen and lawn cuttings from the yard. Decay means to break down.

3. Reduce, Reuse, and Recycle are the three Rs in the solution to the garbage problem.

4. Check to see that students identify the purpose of the essay and summarize its significant points. Summaries should be organized in a thoughtful way, with the main reasons for working to reduce garbage and the important details clearly presented.

**page 88**

1. The first paragraph has a strong and direct tone.

2. The writer gives the readers specific suggestions because he or she wants to persuade the readers to make a change in the way they take care of their own garbage.

3. After all the negative information, the writer gives the readers hope that they can do something positive about the problem.

4. In the first paragraph the writer clearly lays out the huge problem facing Americans. The last paragraph repeats the problem but gives the readers a direct message of positive action. This leaves the readers with a feeling that they can do something about the problem of garbage.